Arduino Projects
for Engineers

A Multipurpose Book For All Engineering Branches

Neerparaj Rai

BPB PUBLICATIONS

Distributors:

COMPUTER BOOK CENTRE
12, Shrungar Shopping Centre,
M.G.Road, BENGALURU–560001
Ph: 25587923/25584641

MICRO BOOKS
Shanti Niketan Building,
8, Camac Street, KOLKATA-700017
Ph: 22826518/22826519

DECCAN AGENCIES
4-3-329, Bank Street,
Hyderabad-500195
Ph: 24756967/24756400

MICRO MEDIA
Shop No. 5, Mahendra Chambers,
150 DN Rd. Next to Capital Cinema,
V.T. (C.S.T.) Station, MUMBAI-400 001
Ph: 22078296/22078297

BPB BOOK CENTRE
376 Old Lajpat Rai Market,
Delhi-110006
Ph: 23861747

INFOTECH
G-2, Sidhartha Building,
96, Nehru Place,
New Delhi -110019
Ph: 41619735, 26438245

BPB PUBLICATIONS
20, Ansari Road, Darya Ganj
New Delhi-110002
Ph: 23254990/23254991

Published by Manish Jain for BPB Publications, 20, Ansari Road, Darya Ganj, New Delhi- 110002 and Printed him at Printed at Repro Knowledgecast Limited, Thane

OTHER TITLES INTEREST

Preface

Firstly, thank you for purchasing this book. I hope it will bring out the more innovative and creative part of you. If you have followed all the projects in this book, you are ready to build more exciting applications based on Arduino. Now you can combine two or more projects to create a whole new prototype to showcase your peak abilities.

Your willingness and desire to create interesting projects also inspires me. Remember always, **"Great Ideas Don't Work Unless You Do the Work"**.

I, Neerparaj Rai (Author) would be grateful to receive any suggestions, comments and enquires regarding the book. Please contact me(e-mail): neerparaj_rai@yahoo.co.in.

This book is meant to be educational and helpful to hobbyist, students and beginners to build real time exciting projects. It primarily focuses on Arduino to do things which houses Atmega 328 microcontroller. This book provides knowledge on twenty four projects with the aid of proper wiring diagrams and programs required to complete the project.

It also discusses about the sensors, modules and other discrete components used in each project. Moreover, the book also introduces power electronic devices like Mosfet and Triac for building inverters and AC regulation circuits. Matlab software is also introduced along with its application together with Arduino which is considered to be the main device for all the projects in the book.

The book covers both software and hardware aspects of each project which will give an overall knowledge to the reader. I hope that this book will help students to empower their knowledge to create their own innovative prototypes.

Detailed Contents

Acknowledgements

I appreciate the help of many persons who contributed to this book directly or indirectly. I would like to thank Mr.Bijay Rai, Electrical Engineering Department, SMIT, Sikkim who introduced me to the world of Arduino.

I would also like to thank and offer this work to the love of my parents Mr.M.B.Rai and Mrs.Munna Devi Rai. I am also grateful to my brothers for their encouragement throughout this project. My final acknowledgement goes to all my faculty colleagues who contributed with valuable suggestions for improvement of the book material.

Interview Questions Series

 .Net Interview Questions

By: Shivprasad Koirala

ISBN: 9788183331470

₹330/-

Networking Interview Questions
By: Shivprasad Koirala
Shaam Sheikh

ISBN: 9788183633243

₹270/-

Software Testing
Interview Questions

By: Shivprasad Koirala

ISBN: 9788183332361

₹297/-

Project Management
Interview Questions
By: Shivprasad Koirala
Shaam Sheikh

ISBN: 9788183332576

₹297/-

SQL Server
Interview Questions

By: Shivprasad Koirala

ISBN: 9788183331036

₹297/-

Jave/J2EE
Interview Questions
By: Shivprasad Koirala

ISBN: 9788183331739

₹297/-

SharePoint Interview
Questions & Answers

By: Shivprasad Koirala

ISBN: 978818333092

₹240/-

Interview Questions In C
Programming
By: Yashavant Kanethkar

ISBN: 9788183332934

₹399/-

About The Author

Neerparaj Rai completed his Master's degree in Power Electronics form Sikkim Manipal Institute of Technology in 2014. He is currently working as Lecturer in Dr.B.R.Ambedkar Institute of Technology, Port Blair. He has also contributed several research papers in many reputed journals and conferences. He has been involved in teaching for over 7 years.

Introduction

Few years ago, building circuits was a tedious job which included connections of components such as resistors, capacitors, inductors, transistors etc. If any change was required, the designer had to go through the entire process of removing and rewiring the complete circuit. Arduino helps the designer to implement the changes required through software programs. Programs are easier to modify than hardware and also saves a lot of time.

Before the advent of Arduino, building a project meant starting from scratch and connecting one component at a time. This restricted the beginners from learning and creating exciting projects. Even for designing simple prototypes, people required extensive knowledge and even help from experts. Nowadays, microcontrollers have become cheaper and easier to use. This opens the way for creation of better prototypes in short period of time.

After working on Arduino, I realized how hobbyist and designers could use it to create innovative and crazy projects. So this book tries to explain things in such a way that might drive engineers crazy. With Arduino, a hobbyist can learn about the basic of electronics and their operations. One can instantly start building projects within minimum time and learn about the microcontroller and its programming. The book is designed to help the beginners to quickly understand and build innovative projects. The book also provides full schematics and all the relevant information regarding every component used in the projects. This book is written for the Arduino designers and students.

With the Arduino board, we can build projects controlled from a computer. The book will show how to interface and control devices from computer through an Arduino board. The book provides all the necessary details about the electronic devices used in the projects along with complete schematic diagrams for every project. For each project we begin with project description and discuss about the hardware components used in the project. At the end, each chapter provides the Arduino sketch (program) required to successfully run the project. With Arduino a whole new range of projects can be built from blinking an LED to flying a quad-copter. Computer controlled projects can also be easily designed using Arduino board.

There are several Arduino products available. All the products are different and are suitable for different types of application. There are currently 19 products available and all can be programmed from the same Arduino IDE. In this book we use the Arduino UNO board for all the projects.

Arduino basically consists of two components (i) hardware, a blue coloured board and ii) software, the program which controls the working of the board.

Arduino is a single board microcontroller which consists of Atmega 328 microcontroller, I/O circuits and RAM. The microcontroller on the Arduino board needs to be programmed via a USB cable. This is the most important advantage of Arduino, that we can directly program the microcontroller on the Arduino board from the computer. Earlier we required a separate programmer to program the microcontroller to perform any task. The board can be powered through the USB connection with the computer or from a 7-12V battery. Once the program is uploaded, the board can be disconnected from the computer to make the board work independently.

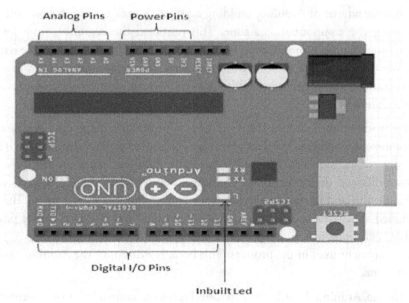

From the figure above, we can see that there are two rows of connectors on the sides of the board. On one side of the board, 14 digital I/O pins are available. On the other side, 6 analogue I/O pins and power supply pins are available. Other technical specifications of the Arduino UNO board are listed below.

Arduino UNO Specifications

Parameter	Value
Operating Voltage	5V
Input Voltage	7-12V
Digital I/O Pins	14
Analog I/O Pins	6
DC Current per I/O Pin	40mA
DC Current for 3.3V Pin	50mA
Flash Memory	32KB
SRAM	2KB
EEPROM	1KB
Clock Speed	16MHz
Size	2.7 × 2.1 inches

The Arduino software development environment is free to download from www. Arduino.cc and requires no lengthy registration procedures. It is a multiplatform environment i.e. it can run on Windows, Macintosh and Linux. Whenever the reader requires additional information, the Arduino web site at www.Arduino.cc can be visited which offers easy to learn tutorials.

The core language used in the Arduino development environment is the C computer programming language. C uses a procedural language syntax that needs to be processed by a compiler to convert high level code to machine level instructions. To make the programming easy for the beginners, the Arduino team has developed many standard Arduino libraries that provide simple set of functions to be used.

The Arduino software development environment is basically used to write, edit, compile and upload your Arduino source code to the interface board. The Arduino software, also called integrated development environment (IDE) allows us to write and easily upload the programs to our Arduino board.

After downloading the Arduino IDE from website: www.Arduino.cc/en/Main/ Software, you need to decompress the downloaded folder on your computer desktop. Open the decompressed folder and launch the exe file shown below.

In case the Java is not previously installed in your computer, install it from website page http://www.java.com/en/download/. You need not follow any installation process and directly open the IDE by clicking on the Arduino exe file. After opening the IDE, it looks similar to the one shown below.

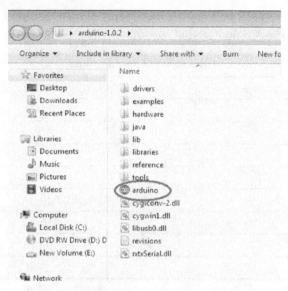

Additional libraries are required for some chapters which are available online. Download the particular library and place the decompressed folder inside the libraries folder of the Arduino software. Following are the list of libraries required.

Chapter title	Chapter Number	Library
Dot Matrix Display	11	LedControl.h
Infrared Remote Control	17	IRremote.h
SD Card Data Logger	18	SD.h
SD Card Data Logger	18	dht11.h

The Arduino IDE provides a graphical interface in which you can write your code, debug it, compile it and upload it to the Arduino board.

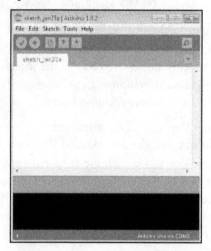

The six icons on the top of the IDE helps you perform different tasks as mentioned below (from left to right).

1. **Verify (check symbol):** This evaluates the code and shows up the errors.

2. **Upload (right-side arrow):** This compiles and uploads your code to the Arduino board.

3. **New (small blank page):** This creates a new blank sketch.

4. **Open (up arrow):** This opens a list of all sketches already existing.

5. **Save (down arrow):** This saves your sketch.

6. **Serial Monitor (small magnifying glass):** This provides the serial monitoring of live data form the Arduino board.

Installing Arduino Driver

At this point you might be familiar with Arduino and its advantages. So it's time to have the Arduino hardware with you as we start with the process of installing the Arduino driver. The process of driver installation for Windows XP and above versions will be discussed.

Steps:

1. Connect the Arduino board to your computer COM port using a USB cable.

2. Click on Start Menu and right click on Computer. Go to 'Manage' option which opens a Management window. Finally open 'Device Manager' on which you can see that your Arduino board is identified as an 'Unknown device'.

3. Next, right click on the 'Unknown device' and choose option 'Update software'.

4. A window opens up and you need to choose 'Browse my computer for driver software' option.

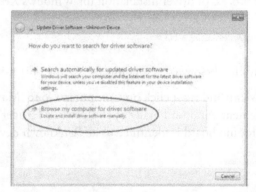

5. Now navigate to the decompressed Arduino software folder and choose the 'drivers' option.

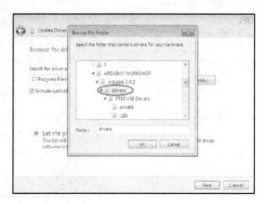

6. On being asked, choose the option 'Install this driver software anyway'.

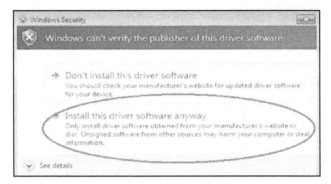

7. After sometime, Windows will finally finish the driver installation and a window appears as shown below.

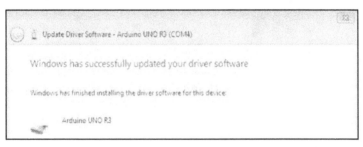

Now on going back to the Device Manager window, you'll see that a serial port number is assigned to your Arduino board. You need to remember that serial port number for further settings later on.

Before moving on with the first project work, open the Arduino IDE and go to 'Tools'. Choose 'Board' and select 'Arduino Uno'.

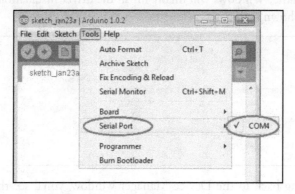

Next you need to go to 'Tools' and select the 'Serial Port' to which the Arduino board is connected.

Now it's time to start with the first project!!

Led Blink

Here we will try to switch on and off a simple LED (Light Emitting Diode) for a time delay of one second each. It a basic experiment and no other components are required except an Arduino board and a USB cable to connect the Arduino board with the computer. All the Arduino boards have an inbuilt LED connected to digital pin 13 as shown in the figure 1.1, so for testing purpose we will be using it for this project.

Components

- Arduino board
- USB Cable

Project 1.1: Turning Inbuilt LED ON and OFF

As our very first project let us try to turn the LED at digital pin 13 which is the inbuilt LED on the Arduino board ON and OFF. Next we will discuss about the Arduino program required to be uploaded to the Arduino board. The program once uploaded, the microcontroller on the Arduino board turns the LED ON and OFF at a time interval of one second.

Explanation:

Every Arduino sketch begins with declaring the constants used in the coding. Here, an integer 'LED' is declared to which value '13' is assigned. An Arduino sketch always comprises of two functions i.e. 'setup' and 'loop' functions. The statements inside 'setup' function will only be executed once, when the program starts. The statements inside 'loop' function will be executed repeatedly, similar to a while loop with null condition.

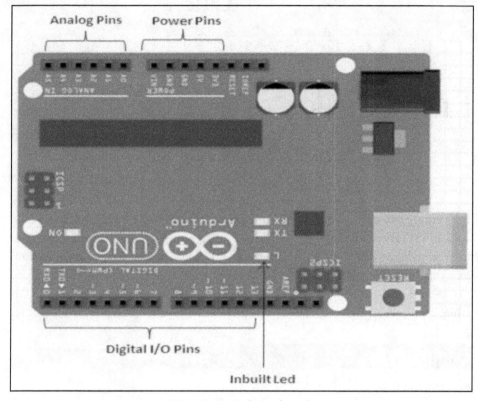

Figure 1.1: Arduino board

Inside the setup function, pin '13' is declared as an 'OUTPUT' pin as we will observe the blinking of inbuilt LED connected to digital pin '13'. As we want to switch on and off the LED at a time delay of one second, pin '13' is made digital 'HIGH' with the statement '*digitalWrite(LED, HIGH)*'. A 'delay' command takes an argument in milliseconds, so '*delay(1000)*' gives a delay of one second and keeps the LED ON for one second. After a delay of one second, '*digitalWrite(LED, LOW)*' statement makes the LED go OFF and waits for a second till LED goes ON again. The statements inside the loop function gets executed repeatedly which makes the LED go ON and OFF continuously as long as the Arduino board is powered.

Write the following program on the Arduino IDE and upload. Observe the blinking of the LED.

Program:

```
int LED = 13;

void setup(){              //setup routine runs once
 pinMode(LED, OUTPUT);     //initialize pin 13 as output
}

void loop() {
 digitalWrite(LED, HIGH);  //turns inbuilt LED on
 delay(1000);
 digitalWrite(LED, LOW);   //turns inbuilt LED off
 delay(1000);
}
// end
```

Led with Push Button

Now, we shall try to switch ON and OFF a LED using a push button. The condition is that the LED should remain on as long as the push button is pressed. In this project, an external LED is used instead of the inbuilt LED at digital pin '13'. A LED functions similar to a diode, so one needs to take care of its orientation on the breadboard. 1kΩ resistance is used to limit the current through the LED to small value i.e. less than 20mA.

Components

- Arduino board

- Push button

- LED

- Resistances (10kΩ and 1kΩ)

- Breadboard

Project 2.1: LED control through Push Button

Digital pins '3' and '12' are used as input and output pins respectively. A resistance of 10kΩ is used as a pull down resistor for the switch. When the push button is pressed, a digital high signal (+5V) appears across digital pin '3' of the Arduino. When the push button is released, pin '3' gets connected to ground. So, if we are able to read the signal at digital pin '3' we shall be able to know the status of the push button. Digital pin '12' is connected to an LED in series with a 1kΩ resistance.

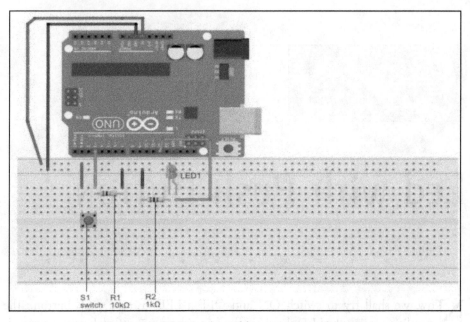

Figure 2.1: LED with pushbutton wiring diagram

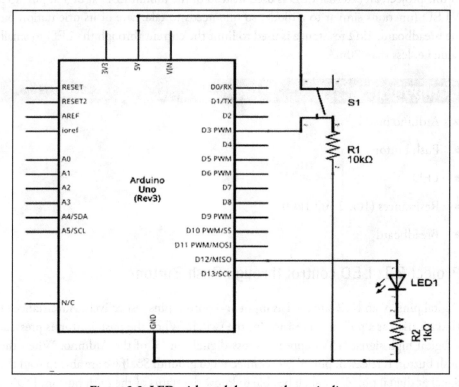

Figure 2.2: LED with push button schematic diagram

Explanation:

Two integer constants 'switchPin' and 'LEDPin' are initialised with values '3' and '12'. Therefore, the setup function declares the digital pins '3' and '12' as 'INPUT' and 'OUTPUT' pins respectively. We need to digitally read pin '3', to check the current status of the push button i.e. whether it is pressed or not. A variable 'switchState' is declared to read the current state of the switch. If the push button is pressed, variable 'switchState' becomes 'HIGH' and thereby the output pin '12' is made digital 'HIGH' else pin '12' is set to digital 'LOW'.

Program:

```
int switchPin=3;      //pin to which switch is connected
int LEDPin=12;        //pin to which LED is connected
int switchState = 0; //variable to read the state of the
switch

void setup() {
 pinMode(switchPin,INPUT);  //initialize pin 3 as input
 pinMode(LEDPin,OUTPUT);    //initialize pin 12 as output
}

void loop() {
switchState = digitalRead(switchPin); //read the state of the
switch
 if(switchState ==HIGH)      //if the switch is pressed
 {
  digitalWrite(LEDPin,HIGH); //turn on LED
 }
 else                        //if the switch is not pressed
 {
  digitalWrite(LEDPin,LOW);  //turn on LED
 }
}
//end
```

Analog Input

There are six analog input pins in Arduino Uno board namely from A0 to A5 (refer figure 1.1). In Arduino Mega you can find sixteen analog pins from A0 to A15 and eight analog pins are available in Arduino Nano. Analog pins are used when we want to read or write variable voltage from 0V to 5V. All the Arduino boards consists of 10 bit ADC (Analog to Digital Converter) i.e. 0V will be read be read as '0' and 5V will be read as '1023' by the microcontroller in the Arduino board. All the voltage values between 0v to 5V will lie in the range '0'to '1023'.

Potentiometer is used as voltage divider such that when the knob of the potentiometer is rotated, variable dc voltage can be read by the microcontroller in the Arduino board through any of the analog pins.

Components

- Arduino board
- Potentiometer (10kΩ)
- Breadboard

Project 3.1: Reading position of a Potentiometer

This project demonstrates reading of analog input on analog pin 0 and viewing the same in the serial monitor. The centre pin of the potentiometer is connected to the analog pin A0 and one side pin (either one) to ground and the other side pin to +5V. As seen in the schematic diagram, the voltage value to the analog pin A0 is varied as the potentiometer is rotated either clockwise or anticlockwise. As the variable point of the potentiometer is moved towards the GND terminal, the voltage value appearing at the analog pin A0 is decreased and the voltage value increases as the variable point is moved towards the +5V terminal. So, this is how the potentiometer is acting as a variable voltage sensor.

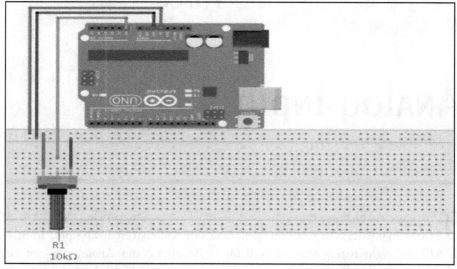

Figure 3.1: Analog input with potentiometer wiring diagram

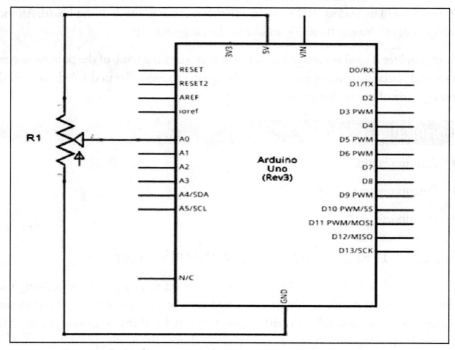

Figure 3.2: Analog input with potentiometer schematic diagram

Explanation:

In the program, analog pin 'A0' is assigned to variable 'sensorPin' and we also take another integer variable 'sensorValue' to get the analog value from analog pin 'AO'. Initially variable 'sensorValue' is set to 0. In setup routine we initialize serial communication at 9600 bits per second. This opens the serial communication between the Arduino board and the PC (computer/laptop) and allows us to view data sent from the microcontroller in the Arduino board through Serial monitor.

The value obtained by '*analogRead()*' at sensor pin 'A0' is placed in variable 'sensorValue' and is simultaneously printed to the Serial monitor. After this the program pauses for 500 milli seconds and the loop routine runs over and over again. To observe the result, open the serial monitor by clicking on the icon as shown below.

Observe the result in the serial monitor which will look similar to the one shown below. We will get a reading of '0' when the potentiometer is at the minimum position and reading of '1023' at maximum position. For further details on serial communication the reader may refer to chapter 15.

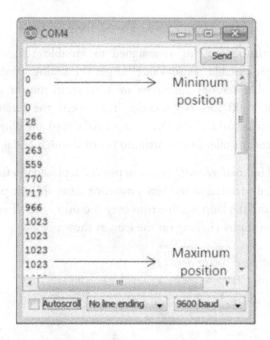

Program:

```
int sensorPin = A0;  // analog input pin for the potentiometer
int sensorValue = 0; // variable to store the value

void setup()
{
  Serial.begin(9600); // Open serial communication between
Arduino and Computer
  }

void loop()
{
  sensorValue = analogRead(sensorPin); // read the value
from potentiometer
  Serial.println(sensorValue); // print out the value you
read
  delay(500); //wait for half a second before reading again
  }
//end
```

h a p t e r   **Four**

Photo-Resistor

A Light Dependent Resistor (LDR) or a photo resistor is a device whose resistivity is a function of the incident electromagnetic radiation or in other words, photo resistor changes it resistance with the ambient light in the room. Hence, they are light sensitive devices. They are also called as photo conductors, photo conductive cells or simply photocells. They are made up of semiconductor materials having high resistance. As the light on the photo-resistor increases, its resistance decreases and vice versa. If we hook up the photo-resistor with a fixed resistance in voltage divider circuit, we can essentially feed into the analog input of the Arduino a voltage that varies with the light in the room. The most commonly used symbol to indicate a photo resistor is shown in figure 4.1 below.

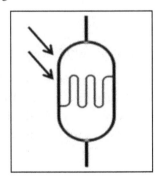

Figure 4.1: Photo resistor symbol

When light falls i.e. when the photons fall on the device, the electrons in the valence band of the semiconductor material are excited to the conduction band. These photons in the incident light should have energy greater than the band gap of the semiconductor material to make the electrons jump from the valence band to the conduction band. Hence when light having enough energy is incident on the device more & more electrons are excited to the conduction band which results in large number of charge carriers. The result of this process is that more and more current starts flowing and hence it is said that the resistance of the device has decreased.

Photo resistors are light dependent devices whose resistance decreases when light falls on them and increases in the dark. When a light dependent resistor is kept in dark, its resistance is very high. This resistance is called as dark resistance. It can be as high as 1kΩ and if the device is allowed to absorb light its resistance will decrease drastically. When light is incident on a photocell it usually takes about 8 to 12ms for the change in resistance to take place, while it takes seconds for the resistance to rise back again to its initial value after removal of light. This phenomenon is called as resistance recovery rate.

Photo resistors have low cost and simple structure. They are often used as light sensors. They are used when there is a need to detect absences or presences of light like in a camera light meter. Used in street lamps, alarm clock, burglar alarm circuits, light intensity meters etc.

Components

- Arduino board
- Resistance (10kΩ)
- Photo-resistor
- Breadboard

Project 4.1 : Photo Resistor as Light Sensor

A voltage divider circuit using a photo-resistor and a 10kΩ resistor is build. The analog input to the Arduino board is fed through pin 'A0'. Therefore the analog input reads the voltage across the 10kΩ resistance. As the light intensity on the sensor increases, the analog input voltage to the Arduino increases and vice versa.

Explanation:

Whenever we first hook up a sensor with the Arduino we need to check the range of the data being received from the sensor. To do this we need to read the analog pin 'A0' and print the sensor value to the serial monitor. The program is similar to that of project 3.1.

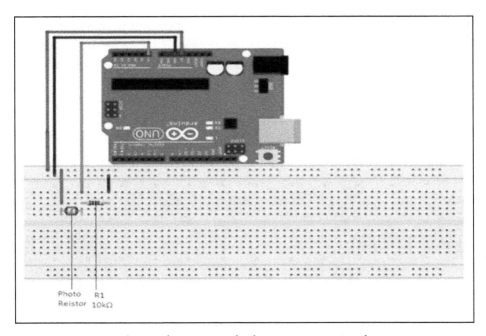

Figure 4.2: Analog input with photo-resistor wiring diagram

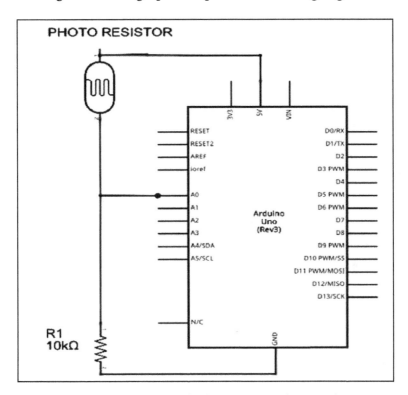

Figure 4.3: Analog input with photo-resistor schematic diagram

In figure 4.2 the analog voltage to the Arduino will decrease as we try to reduce the light falling on the photo-resistor. As we have placed a 10kΩ with the photo-resistor, here we are getting a range of approximately '500' i.e. '1020' when the photo-resistor is not covered and approximately '680' when the photo-resistor is fully covered from ambient light. These values are received by the microcontroller through ADC (Analog to Digital Converter) with 10 bit resolution. The range of '500' can be further improved using other values of fixed resistance in the voltage divider circuit. The result in the Serial monitor is shown below.

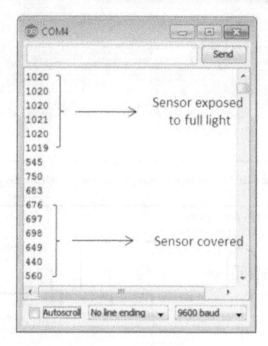

Program:

```
int sensorPin = A0; // analog input pin for reading the
                    sensor value
int sensorValue = 0; // variable to store the value


void setup()
{
  Serial.begin(9600); //opens serial communication between
                    Arduino and PC

}
```

```
void loop()
{
 sensorValue = analogRead(sensorPin); // read the sensor
value from voltage divider circuit
 Serial.println( sensorValue); //display the sensor value
in the serial monitor
 delay(500); //wait for half a second
 }
//end
```

Photo-resistor with LED

This project is an extension of Project 4.1. We will try to turn ON and OFF the LED depending upon the light falling on the photo-resistor. LED is connected to digital pin 11 in series with 1kΩ resistance so as to limit the current.

Components

- Arduino board

- Resistance (10kΩ and 1kΩ)

- Photo-resistor

- Light emitting diode

- Breadboard

Project 5.1: Photo Resistor as Light Intensity Detector

In project 4.1, we received an analog value of '1020' when the photo resistor was exposed to full light and '680' when the photo resistor was covered. So here we need to write the program such that the LED connected to digital pin 11 turns ON when the reading of the analog voltage goes below '700' i.e. to show that the intensity of the light has decreased in the room and additional LED light is turned ON. Similarly the LED should be turned OFF when the reading of the analog voltage becomes greater than '1000'.

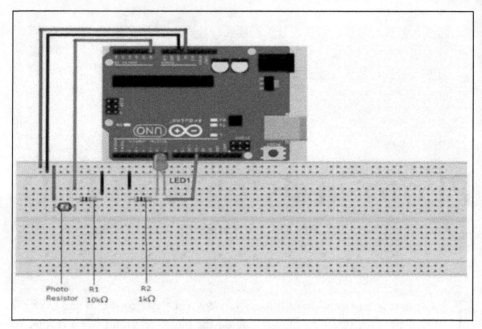

Figure 5.1: Photo resistor with LED wiring diagram

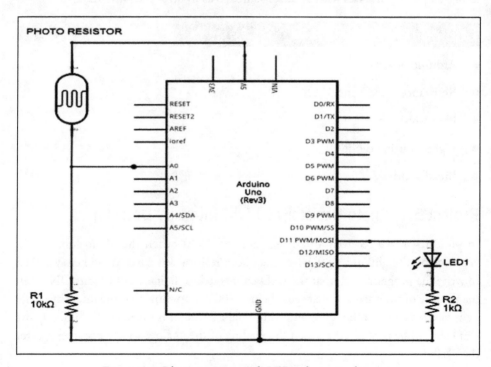

Figure 5.2: Photo resistor with LED schematic diagram

Explanation:

Analog pin 'A0' is used as analog input pin to read the voltage across the 10kΩ fixed resistor. An integer variable 'sensorValue' is declared which will be used to store the integer value of the analog voltage at pin 'A0'. Another integer variable 'LED' is assigned with value '11' to which LED is connected. Digital pin '11' is used as 'OUTPUT' pin which is declared inside 'setup' function.

The voltage at the analog pin 'A0'is continuously read and stored in the variable 'sensorValue'. In project 4.1, we had seen that the variable 'sensorValue' was '680' when the photo-resistor was covered i.e. we can consider the room is dark. So if the variable 'sensorValue' is less than '700', LED at digital pin 11 is turned ON using command 'digitalWrite(LED, HIGH)'. Else if the variable 'sensorValue' is greater than '1000', which means the room has sufficient light and LED is thereby turned OFF with command 'digitalWrite(LED, LOW)'.

Program:

```
int sensorPin = A0;      // analog input pin for reading the
sensor value
int sensorValue = 0;     // variable to store the value
int LED = 11;            // pin 11 has an LED connected

void setup()
{
  pinMode(LED, OUTPUT); // initialize the digital pin 11 as
an output
  }
void loop()
{
  sensorValue = analogRead(sensorPin);   // read the value
from the sensor
if(sensorValue<700)                       //if sensor value
is less than 700
{
  digitalWrite(LED, HIGH);                //switch LED on
}
else if(sensorValue>1000)                 //if sensor value
is greater than 1000
{
```

```
digitalWrite(LED, LOW); //switch LED on
}
}
//end
```

Project 5.2: Photo Resistor as variable Light intensity Detector

Further to the extension of Project 5.1 instead of just turning the LED ON and OFF depending upon the intensity of light falling on the photo-resistor, we can also change the illumination of the LED. In other words, we can increase the illumination of LED as the light falling on the photo-resistor decreases and vice-versa.

Explanation:

To do this, we need to use 'constrain' and 'map' function. 'Constrain' function limits a variable to be within a range. What the 'constrain' function does here is that if the variable 'sensorValue' is less than '700', it will be equal to '700' and if 'sensorValue' becomes greater than '1000', it will be made equal to '1000'. As 'map' function does not constrain values to within a range, 'constrain' function should be used before 'map' function.

In order to change the illumination of LED connected at digital pin '11', we need to use 'analogWrite' function. Basically 'analogWrite' function uses digital means to get analog results by using PWM (Pulse Width Modulation) technique. PWM is a digital control technique to create a square wave, a signal switched between ON and OFF. This ON and OFF pattern can simulate average voltages in between full ON (+5 volts) and OFF (0 volts) by changing the portion of the time the signal is ON for a frequency of 500Hz. At 500Hz if you repeat this ON-OFF pattern fast enough with an LED for example, the result is as if the signal is a steady voltage between 0 and +5V, thereby controlling the brightness of the LED. A call to function 'analogWrite' is on a scale of 0-255, such that '*analogWrite(255)*' requests a 100% duty cycle and '*analogWrite(127)*' is a 50% duty cycle and so on.

But the problem is that analog read has 10 bit resolution having a range from 0 to 1023 (2^{10}) whereas analog write is on a scale of 0 to 255 (2^8) with 8 bit resolution. Therefore we need to use 'map' function to reset the range for the variable 'sensorValue'.A 'Map' function remaps a number from one range to another. According to the statement '*map(sensorValue, 700, 1000, 255, 0)*', value '760' will be made equal to '255' which means LED will be fully ON when the photo-resistor is completely covered. Similarly, value '1000' will be made equal to '0' which indicates that LED will be OFF when the photo-resistor is left un-covered and the in between values from '700' to '1000' will be mapped accordingly from '255' to '0' so as to get an inverse relation.

Program:

```
int sensorPin = A0;      // analog input pin for reading the
sensor value
int sensorValue = 0;     // variable to store the value
int LED = 11;            // pin 11 has an LED connected

void setup()
{
 pinMode(LED, OUTPUT); // initialize the digital pin 11 as
an output
 }

void loop()
{
 sensorValue = analogRead(sensorPin);
 sensorValue = constrain(sensorValue, 760, 950); //constrain
the sensor value between 760 and 950
 int level = map(sensorValue, 760, 950, 255, 0); //map the
sensor value between 255 and 0
 analogWrite(LED, level); //write mapped analog value to pin
11
 }
//end
```

DC Motor with Transistor

In this project, you will learn how to control a small DC motor using an Arduino and a transistor. You will also use an Arduino analog output (PWM) to control the speed of the motor by sending a number between 0 and 255 from the digital pin of Arduino.

DC motor is a motor that runs on DC voltage. The toy cars and robots may have one or more DC motors to move their wheels or arms. In fact in robotics it is the most popular one. It is composed of a permanent cylindrical magnets and a wire wound shaft. It has two power connections to apply the voltage. One is termed as positive and the other is negative. If we apply at least 1.5 volts DC to the motor it will start moving in a clockwise direction. If we reverse the polarity then it will move in the opposite direction.

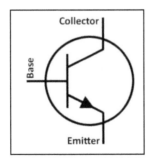

Figure 6.1: Transistor 2N2222 pin diagram

Firstly we will try to turn ON and OFF the DC motor with the help of an n-p-n transistor 2N2222. An n-p-n transistor has three pins namely emitter, base and collector as shown in figure 6.1.

The technical specifications of transistor 2N2222 are listed below.

Table 6.1: Transistor 2N2222 specifications.

Sl.No	Parameter	Rated Value
1.	Collector-Emitter Voltage (VCE)	40 V
2.	Emitter-Base Voltage (VBE)	5 V
3.	Collector Current	0.8 A
4.	Turn-On Time	35 nsec

In a transistor, current can flow through collector to emitter depending on the state of the base pin with respect to the emitter. If the base is at higher potential than emitter, we have current flowing from collector to emitter. Current flow from collector to emitter is restricted if base is grounded. So, basically here transistor is used as a switch depending on the voltage level in the base pin. The advantage of using a transistor to turn ON and OFF the motor is to isolate the motor from Arduino because Arduino cannot drive sufficient current to drive the motor. Also we will be able to connect the motor to higher voltages i.e. 9V which will make the motor run faster.

We also need to use a separate battery pack of 9V to power up the motor because the DC motor is likely to use more power than an Arduino digital output can handle directly. If we try to connect the motor directly to an Arduino digital pin, there is a good chance that it could damage the Arduino. Small transistor like the 2N2222 can be used as a switch that uses just a little current from the Arduino digital output to control the much bigger current of the motor.

Components

- Arduino board
- DC Motor (9V-12V)
- Transistor (2N2222)
- Diode (IN4001)
- Resistor (1kΩ)
- Potentiometer (10kΩ)
- Battery (9V)
- Breadboard

Project 6.1: DC Motor Control using Transistor

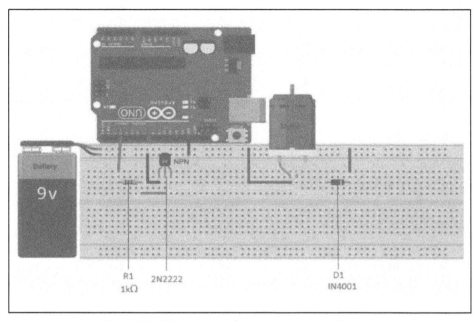

Figure 6.2: DC motor with transistor wiring diagram

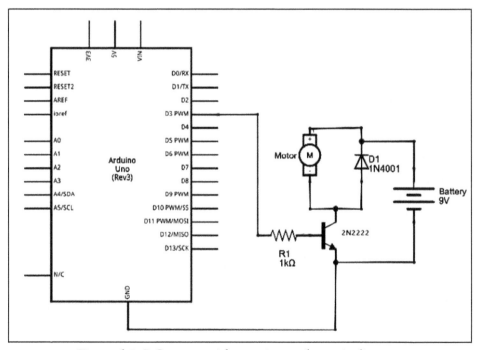

Figure 6.3: DC motor with transistor schematic diagram

The base of transistor is connected to digital pin '3' of Arduino which is capable of PWM control through a 1kΩ resistor. The function of 1kΩ resistance is to isolate the Arduino board from 9V signal. A diode is placed across the motor so as to protect the Arduino and transistor from noise and spike signals which are generally created by the motor. When you turn the power off to a motor, you get a negative spike of voltage that can damage your Arduino or the transistor. The diode protects against this, by shorting out any such reverse current from the motor.

Explanation:

Digital pin '3' is termed as 'motorPin' and is configured as 'OUTPUT' pin. The motor turns on when a 'HIGH' command is sent to pin '3' and the motor keeps running for two seconds. To turn the motor off, a 'LOW' command is sent to pin '3' and the motor remains off for another two seconds.

The ON and OFF control of the motor can also be achieved by incorporating a push button and thereby controlling the motor with it. The reader can perform the said project and edit the program accordingly.

Program:

```
int motorPin = 3; //declare the pin to which the base of the
transistor is connected

void setup()
{
  pinMode(motorPin, OUTPUT); //initialize pin 3 as output
}
void loop() {
  digitalWrite(motorPin, HIGH); // turn motor on
  delay(2000); // wait for two second
  digitalWrite(motorPin, LOW); // turn motor off
  delay(2000); // wait for two second
}
//end
```

Project 6.2: DC Motor Speed Control using a Potentiometer

To go further with the operation of DC motor, we will now learn to control the speed of the motor using PWM, which we generated last time. The project uses a potentiometer of 10kΩ to control the speed of the motor. As we rotate the pot in clockwise direction, the speed of the motor will increase and when the pot is rotated in anti-clockwise direction, the speed of the motor decreases.

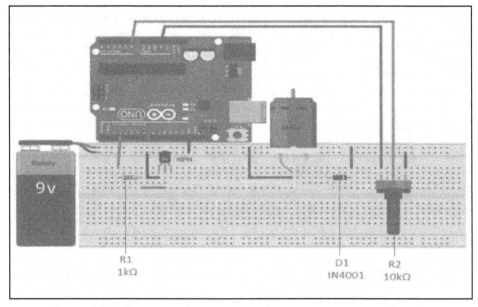

Figure 6.4: DC motor with transistor and potentiometer wiring diagram

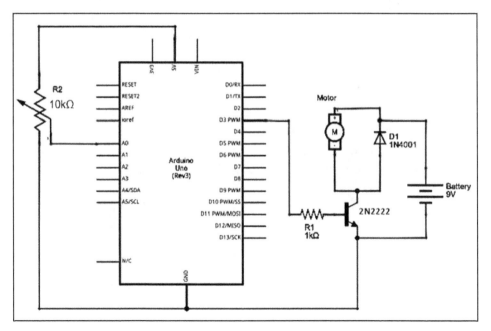

Figure 6.5: DC motor with transistor and potentiometer schematic diagram

Explanation:

We are using 'analogRead' to read the position of potentiometer from analog pin 'A0'. The speed of the motor is being changed by using 'analogWrite' command at digital pin '3' which is capable of PWM control. In others words, we will be using PWM to control the motor speed which requires analog voltage. A square-wave of 50% duty-cycle i.e. goes 'ON' for 50% of the cycle and goes 'OFF' for the rest of the cycle have an average voltage of half as much as the maximum voltage of the pulse. Therefore, reducing the output voltage across the motor, this in turn makes the motor run slower than at maximum voltage.

Since the analog reading will be between 0 and 1023 and the analog output needs to be between 0 and 255, we are again using map function to reset the range. Speed control for DC motors of higher ratings can be obtained by choosing a transistor or MOSFET of higher current and voltage rating than the motor.

Program:

```
int motorPin = 3; //declare the pin to which the base of the
transistor is connected
int potPin = A0; // analog input pin for reading the
potentiometer value
int potValue=0;   //variable to store the potentiometer value
void setup()
 {
 pinMode(motorPin, OUTPUT);   //initialize pin 3 as output
 }
void loop()
 {
 potValue = analogRead(potPin); // Read pot position
 int speedLevel = map(potValue,0, 1023, 0, 255); // Map the
potValue from 0-1023 to 0-255
 analogWrite(motorPin,speedLevel ); //Set the speed of motor
 }
//end
```

DC Motor with L293d

We need to know that Arduino board can only provide 40mA current through its digital pins, which is not sufficient to run motors which require more than 40mA current. To use Arduino for such type of control applications we usually use either a MOSFET, transistors or some other integrated circuit (IC) chip.

In this project we will learn how to control directional motion of a simple DC motor using Arduino Uno board with the help of a motor driving integrated circuit chip L293D. In the second part of this project we will also learn to control the speed of the motor using PWM, more or less similar to project 6.2.

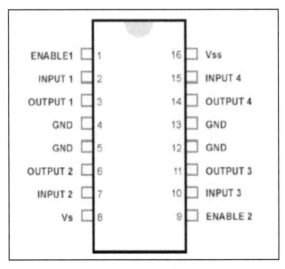

Figure 7.1: L293D pin diagram

L239D is a 16-bit IC, with 2-channel motor control or in other words, you can control and move two motors using this IC both in clockwise and anti-clockwise direction. Each channel has a separate enable pin, 2 input pins, 2 ground pins, and 2 output pins. We will use only one channel for this project to control a single DC motor. There is one supply voltage pin (Vs) and a logic reference voltage pin (Vss). Output 1 and Output 2 will be connected to positive and negative terminal of the DC motor. The pin configuration of the IC is shown below.

The electrical characteristics of L293D per channel are:

Table 7.1: L293D per channel specifications

Sl.No	Symbol	Parameter	Value
1.	Vs	Supply Voltage	24V
2.	Vss	Logic Supply Voltage	5V
3.	Ven	Enable Voltage	5V
4.	Io	Output Current	600mA
5.	P	Power Dissipation	4W

This is a very useful chip. It can actually control two motors independently. We are just using half the chip in this project but the connection on both the half will be similar.

Components

- Arduino board
- DC Motor (9V-12V)
- L293D IC
- Potentiometer (10kΩ)
- Battery (9V)
- Breadboard

Project 7.1: DC motor direction control using L293D

The aim of the project is to control the direction of rotation of DC motor using L293D driver IC. Digital pin '2' and '6' of Arduino needs to be wired with L293D pins '15' and '10' for direction control. Since we are using the second channel of L293D, ENABLE 2 pin should be set HIGH by wiring it to 5V bus. The logic supply voltage Vss is also wired to 5V bus. All the ground connections need to form a common node.L293D pins OUTPUT 3 and OUTPUT 4 gets connected to motor terminals as indicated in figure 7.2 and 7.3. The positive terminal of the 9V battery to Vs pin of L293D.

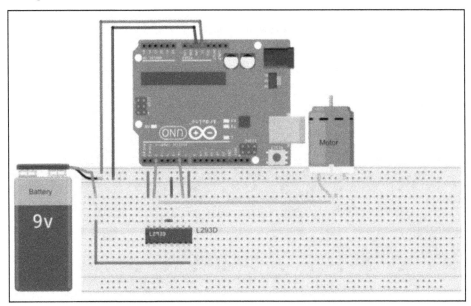

Figure 7.2: DC motor with L293D IC wiring diagram

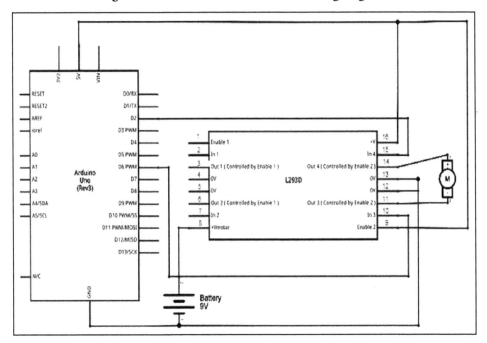

Figure 7.3: DC motor with L293D IC schematic diagram

Explanation:

The program given below controls the direction of rotation of DC motor i.e. the motor will rotate in clockwise direction for two seconds and anti-clockwise direction or reverse for another two seconds and so on.

To do this, INPUT 3 (pin no 10) and INPUT 4 (pin no 15) pins of L293D is connected to digital pins '2' and '6' of Arduino. Depending on the status of digital pins '2' and '6', the motor will run in either direction for which the truth table is given. As seen in the truth table, if both the digital pins connected to the INPUT 3 and INPUT 4 of L293D IC have the same logic than the motor will stop.

Table 7.2: Truth table for direction control

Digital pin '3'	Digital pin '6'	DC Motor
LOW	LOW	STOP
LOW	HIGH	ANTI CLOCKWISE
HIGH	LOW	CLOCKWISE
HIGH	HIGH	STOP

Pins '2' and '6' are declared as output pins in the setup function through variables 'Input_4' and 'Input _3' respectively. Inside the loop function, pin '2' is set 'HIGH' and pin '6' is set 'LOW' which causes the motor to run in clockwise direction followed by a delay of two seconds which keeps the motor running clockwise for the delayed time. After which the status of pins '2' and '6' are interchanged to make the motor reverse its direction and starts running in anti-clockwise direction for another two seconds. As the loop functions continues to run over and over again forever, the same set of operation also continues forever.

Program:

```
int Input_4 = 2;
int Input _3 = 6;

void setup()
{
 pinMode(Input_4, OUTPUT);
 pinMode(Input _3, OUTPUT);
}
void loop()
{
 digitalWrite(Input_4, HIGH); // run motor clockwise
```

```
digitalWrite(Input _3, LOW); // run motor clockwise
delay(2000);  // wait for two second

digitalWrite(Input_4, LOW); // run motor anti-clockwise
digitalWrite(Input_3, HIGH); // run motor anti-clockwise
delay(2000);     // wait for two second
}
//end
```

Project 7.2: DC motor speed control using L293D

Similar to project 6.2, now we want to change the speed of the motor rotating in a fixed direction. We are using a potentiometer as a reference to vary the speed of the DC motor. Analog reading from the potentiometer at analog pin 'A0' is done continuously to keep track of its current position. The speed of the motor is set, by using an 'analogWrite' function to write PWM signal at the ENABLE 2 pin of L293D. If you connect ENABLE 2 pin to GND, the motor will stop irrespective of the status of control pins INPUT 3 and INPUT 4. Enable pin turns everything on and off. This makes it useful for using a PWM output to control the motor speed.

So the ENABLE 2 pin is connected to digital pin '9' of Arduino for PWM control. The duty cycle of the PWM signal at digital pin '9' will vary with the corresponding rotation of the potentiometer connected to analog pin 'A0'.

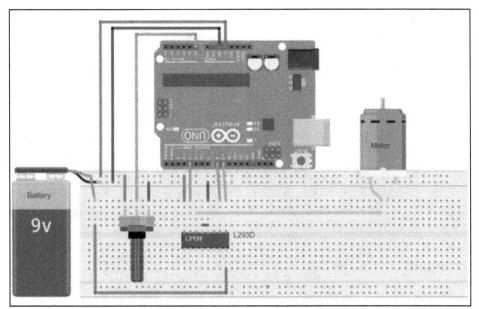

Figure 7.4: DC motor speed regulation with L293D IC wiring diagram

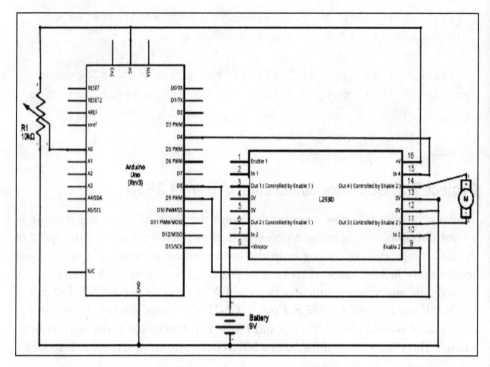

Figure 7.5: DC motor speed regulation with L293D IC schematic diagram

Explanation:

INPUT 4 and INPUT 3 pins of L293D are wired to digital pins '4' and '8' and are digitally fixed at 'HIGH' and 'LOW' status which causes the motor to run only one direction. We do not want to change the direction of the motor, therefore commands 'digitalWrite (Input_4, HIGH)' and 'digitalWrite (Input_3, LOW)' are written inside setup function because the setup function runs only once when the program is initially executed.

Again PWM control is used to regulate the speed of the motor using digital pin '9' which is connected to ENABLE 2 pin of L293D. After each analog reading at analog pin 'A0', the 'potValue' is mapped to a new variable 'speedLevel'. The 'analogWrite' function for 'enablePin' sets the motor to a new speed according to the new position of the potentiometer. For every setting of the potentiometer, the motor starts running at a new speed.

Program:

```
int Input_4 = 4;
int Input_3 = 8;
```

```
int enablePin = 9; //enable pin control through digital pin
9
int potPin = A0; //analog pin A0 for potentiometer reading
int potValue = 0; //variable for analog reading

void setup()
{
pinMode(Input_4, OUTPUT);
pinMode(Input_3, OUTPUT);
digitalWrite(Input_4, HIGH); // run motor clockwise
digitalWrite(Input_3, LOW);  // run motor clockwise
}

void loop()
{
potValue = analogRead(potPin); // Read potentiometer position
int speedLevel = map(potValue,0, 1023, 0, 255); // Map the
potValue from 0-1023 to 0-255
analogWrite(enablePin,speedLevel ); //Set the speed of motor
}

//end
```

SERVOMOTOR

In this project, you will learn how to control a servo motor using an Arduino. Unlike dc motors, with servo motors you can position the motor shaft at a specific position (angle) using control signal. A servo motor consists of a regular dc motor connected to a gear box and a potentiometer that give the feedback for angle position. The motor shaft will hold at this position as long as the control signal is not changed. This is very useful for controlling robot arms, unmanned airplanes control surface or any object that you want it to move at certain angle and stay at its new position.

Components

- Arduino board

- Servo Motor

- Voltage Regulator (IC 7805)

- Potentiometer (10kΩ)

- Capacitors (1μF and 22μF)

- Battery (9V)

- Breadboard

Servos with many different speed, size and torque capabilities are available, but all have 3 wires i.e. power, ground and control. The colour of the leads varies between servo motors, but the red wire is always 5V (power) and GND (ground) will either be black or brown. The other wire is the control wire and this is usually orange or yellow.

The control wires accept the signal which is a pulse-width modulation (PWM) signal which can be easily produced by Arduino board. The Arduino software comes with a servo library that will get you running servo quickly.

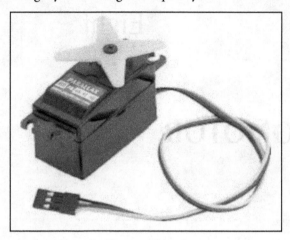

Figure 8.1: Servo Motor

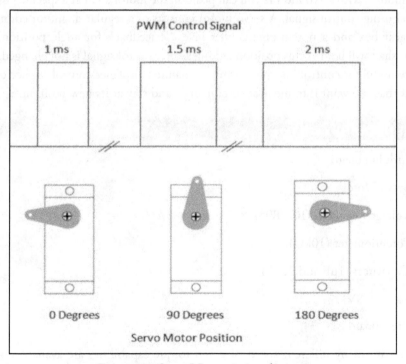

Figure 8.2: Servo Motor timing diagram

The PWM signal to the control wire from your controller tells the servo what angle to turn to. The length of the pulse corresponds to the angle the motor turns to. When the pulse width is less than or equal to 1ms the motor will move to the 0 degree position and hold. When the pulse width is equal 1.5ms the motor will rotate to the 90 degree position and if the pulse width is greater than 1.5 ms the motor will rotate towards the 180 position as shown in the timing diagram. When the motor reaches the desired position it will hold there until next PWM signal of different width is sent. The PWM frequency is fixed at 20ms.

We are using an external source of 9 volts when powering the servo motor because the motor will draw more current than the Arduino can provide under load condition or while connecting multiple motors. Since the rated voltage of the servo motor that are generally available for projects is 5V, we need to regulate the 9V battery voltage down to 5V using a voltage regulator IC 7805.

A 7805 IC is a voltage regulator integrated circuit. It is a member of 78xx series of fixed linear voltage regulator ICs. The voltage source in a circuit may have fluctuations and would not give the fixed voltage output. The voltage regulator IC maintains the output voltage at a constant value.

The maximum value for input to the voltage regulator is 35V. It can provide a constant steady voltage flow of 5V for higher voltage input till the threshold limit of 35V. It regulates a steady output of 5V if the input voltage is in range of 7.2V to 35V. To avoid excess power loss try to maintain the input to 7.2V. The maximum output current that can be drawn from the 7805 IC is 1.5A without overheating.

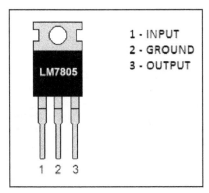

Figure 8.3: IC 7805 pin diagram

A general 5V voltage regulation circuit with decoupling capacitors is shown below. C1 capacitor is known as bypass capacitor and is employed to bypass extremely tiny duration spikes to the ground without any damage to the other components. C2 is known as a filter capacitor employed in the circuit to steady the slow alterations in the output voltage. Raising the value of the capacitor enlarges the stabilization furthermore and declining the value of the capacitor decreases the stabilization.

Table 8.1: IC 7805 Pin Description

Pin No	Name	Function
1	Input	Breadboard
2	Ground	Ground 0V
3	Output	Output Voltage 5V (4.8V – 5.2V)

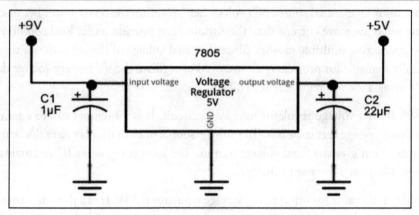

Figure 8.4: 5V Regulation circuit using IC 7805

Project 8.1: Servo Motor Angular Movement Control

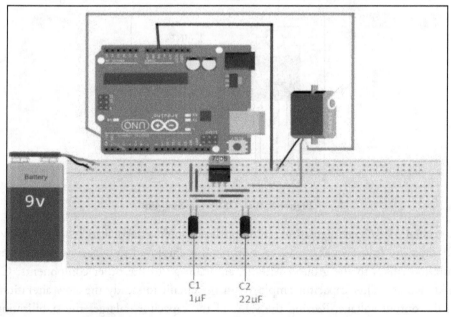

Figure 8.5: Servo motor angular control wiring diagram

The angular limitation of a servo motor is 180 degrees. In this project we shall try to rotate the servo motor from 0 degrees to 180 degrees in steps. According to the wiring diagram in figure 8.5, the input is a 9V battery and the output of 5V from IC 7805 is supplied to servo power terminals. The grounds for Arduino, 9V battery and servo motor needs to have a common node. The control pin of the servo needs to be connected to one of the PWM outputs of the Arduino UNO (Pins: 3, 5, 6, 9, 10 and 11). Pin 3 will be used for this application note.

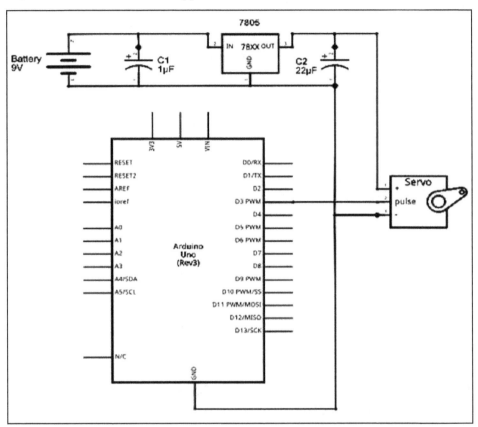

Figure 8.6: Servo motor angular control schematic diagram

Explanation:

'Servo.h' library is included in the program to use inbuilt commands to control the servo motor. First we need to create a servo object which makes things simpler when it comes to controlling more than one servo motor. The servo object 'myServo' is thereby attached to digital pin '3' inside setup function. The void loop contains a 'for' loop, to rotate servo from 0 to 180 degrees. Initially the 'for' loop sets the PWM signal output to 1ms and moves the servo motor to 0 degrees. The pulse width is then incremented by 0.11ms each time the loop is entered and the pulse width is written to digital pin '3' of Arduino until the pulse width reaches 2ms i.e. the 180 degree position. There is also a delay of 0.25 sec each time the pulse width is written to pin '3' and before sending the next signal to allow the motor to reach its currently directed position. The delay can be adjusted according to the requirement to increase or decrease the speed of the servo rotation.

Program:

```
#include <Servo.h> //include servo library
Servo myservo;        // create servo object

void setup()
 {
 myservo.attach(3);   // attaches the servo on digital pin 3
 }

void loop()
 {
  for (int i = 0; i <=180; i = i+20)
  {
  myservo.write(i);        // sets the servo position
  delay(250);              // waits for quarter of a second
  }
 }
//end
```

Project 8.2: Servo Motor Angular Movement Control using a Potentiometer

The second portion of the project explains about how we can control the position of the servo by turning the potentiometer. We just need another potentiometer and connect its variable terminal to analog input 'A0'. Connect its end terminals to 5V and GND. We continuously take analog reading from 'A0' and accordingly set the position of the servo. Analog reading gives us a value of between 0 and 1023. As the maximum degree of rotation of servo motor is 180 degrees, we need to scale it down in the range from 0 to 180. Dividing 1023 by six will give us an angle between 0 and 170, which is sufficient to operate servos for most of the applications. One can also use map function which has been introduced in the earlier chapters.

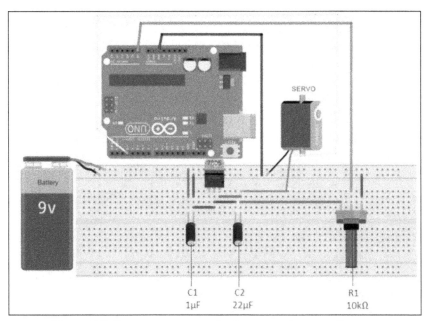

Figure 8.7: Servo motor control using potentiometer diagram

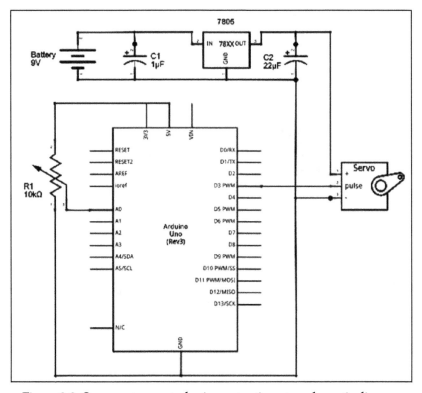

Figure 8.8: Servo motor control using potentiometer schematic diagram

Explanation:

The first step is to include the 'Servo.h' library which contains commands for control of a Servo. An integer variable 'potPin' is initialized with 'A0' to read analog pin 'A0'. The servo control is attached to digital pin '3' of Arduino inside setup function. Analog value read at pin 'A0' showing the potentiometer position is stored in variable 'potValue'. The analog value so read is thereby divided by integer value 6, the reason for which was foresaid. The value so obtained decides servo motor angle. This is achieved by setting the length of the PWM signal output at digital pin '3' on the Arduino board.

Program:

```
#include <Servo.h> //include servo library
Servo myservo;      // create servo object
int potPin = A0;
int potValue = 0;  //variable to store analog value

void setup() {
 myservo.attach(3); // attaches the servo on digital pin 3
}

void loop()
{
  potValue = analogRead(potPin);  //reading potentiometer
position in the range (0 - 1023)
 potValue = potValue/6; // scaling the range down to (0 - 170)
 myservo.write(potValue);  // sets the new servo position
 delay(500);       // waits for half a second
}

//end
```

Nine

LCD Display

L CD modules form a very important part in many Arduino based embedded
system designs. So the knowledge of interfacing LCD to Arduino is very essential
in designing embedded systems. This article is about interfacing a 16×2 LCD to
Arduino. JHD 162A is the LCD module used here. JHD 162A is a 16×2 LCD
module based on the HD 44780 driver from Hitachi. The JHD 162A has 16 pins and
can be operated in 4-bit mode or 8-bit mode. Here we are using the LCD module in
4-bit mode. Firstly we shall display plain text messages on the LCD and then we will
try to incorporate LCD with other useful projects.

Figure 9.1 shows the pin diagram of a 16×2 LCD and the pin description is also given
below.

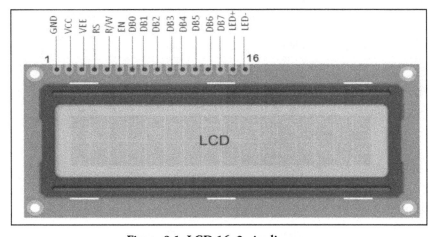

Figure 9.1: LCD 16×2 pin diagram

- **Pin1 (GND):** Ground pin of the LCD module.

- **Pin2 (Vcc):** +5V supply is given to this pin

- **Pin3 (VEE):** Contrast adjustment pin. This is done by connecting the ends of a 10K potentiometer to +5V and ground and then connecting the slider pin to the VEE pin. The voltage at the VEE pin defines the contrast. The normal setting is between 0.4 and 0.9V. To keep the things simple we will connect this pin to ground which gives a good contrast.

- **Pin4 (RS):** It is the register select pin. The JHD162A has two registers namely command register and data register. Logic HIGH at RS pin selects data register and logic LOW at RS pin will select command register. The command register stores the command instructions given to the LCD. A command is an instruction given to LCD to do a predefined task like initializing it, clearing its screen, setting the cursor position, controlling display etc. The data register stores the data to be displayed on the LCD. The data is the ASCII value of the character to be displayed on the LCD.

- **Pin5 (R/W):** Read/Write modes. This pin is used for selecting between read and write modes. Logic HIGH at this pin activates read mode and logic LOW at this pin activates write mode.

- **Pin6 (Enable):** This pin is meant for enabling the LCD module. A HIGH to LOW signal at this pin will enable the module.

- **Pin7 (DB0) to Pin14 (DB7):** These are data pins. The commands and data are put on these pins.

- **Pin15 (LED+):** Anode of the back light LED. In Arduino based projects the back light LED can also be powered from the 3.3V source instead of 5V on the Arduino board.

- **Pin16 (LED–):** Cathode of the back light LED.

Components

- Arduino board
- Liquid Crystal Display (16×2)
- Breadboard

Project 9.1: Displaying Text on LCD Display

The 16x2 LCD is used to display a string of characters. Maximum of 16 characters can be displayed on each row. As we will only be writing data on the LCD, Pin5 (R/W) is set LOW by connecting it to GND. The following table illustrates the connection between LCD and Arduino.

Table 9.1: LCD and Arduino connections

LCD Pins	Arduino Pins
1,3,5 and 16	GND
2, 15	5V
4	3
6	5
11 to 14	9 to 12

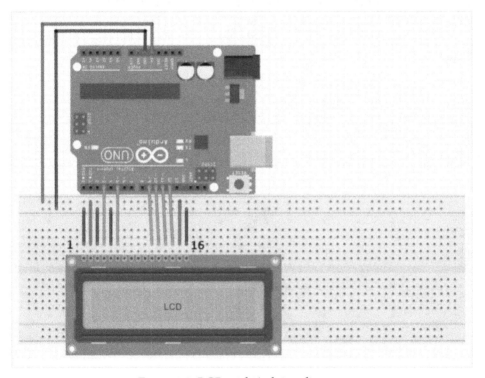

Figure 9.2: LCD with Arduino diagram

Explanation:

Library function 'LiquidCrystal.h' is used for displaying the desired characters on the LCD module. It is readily available with the Arduino user interface and it can be accessed through the "Import library" in the "sketch" tab in the main menu bar. The 'LiquidCrystal.h' provides functions for almost all applications like printing a string, setting the cursor, initializing the LCD, scrolling the display etc.

RS pin of the LCD module is connected to digital pin 3 of the Arduino. R/W pin of the LCD is grounded. Enable pin of the LCD module is connected to digital pin 5 of the Arduino. In this project, the LCD module and Arduino are interfaced in the 4-bit mode. That means only four of the digital input lines (DB4 to DB7 of the LCD are used). This method is very simple, requires less connections and you can almost utilize the full potential of the LCD module. Digital lines DB4, DB5, DB6 and DB7 are interfaced to digital pins 9, 10, 11 and 12 of the Arduino. The Arduino can be powered through the external power jack provided on the board. The Arduino can be also powered from the PC through the USB port. The full program for interfacing LCD to Arduino is shown below.

After the interfacing of LCD is done and the program is uploaded, it will display string 'ARDUINO PROJECT' in the first row and 'LCD INTERFACING' in the second row.

Program:

```
#include<LiquidCrystal.h> //include the library for LCD
LiquidCrystal lcd(3, 5, 9, 10, 11, 12); // sets the
interfacing pins (RS,Enable,D4,D5,D6,D7)

void setup()
{
  lcd.begin(16, 2); // initializes the 16x2 LCD
}
void loop()
{
  lcd.setCursor(0,0); //sets the cursor at row 0 column 0
  lcd.print("ARDUINO PROJECT"); // prints 16x2 LCD MODULE
  lcd.setCursor(0,1); //sets the cursor at row 1 column 0
  lcd.print("LCD INTERFACING"); // prints HELLO WORLD
}
//end
```

Project 9.2: Scrolling text on LCD display

In case when the string to be displayed is long or more than 16 characters, we need to scroll the string left to right. The same is achieved by the program given below.

Explanation:

A simple program for scrolling a text on the LCD using Arduino is shown here. This is done using the 'scroll()' function. For example the function 'lcd.scrollDisplayRight()'

will scroll the display to right and the function '*lcd.scrollDisplayLeft()*' will scroll the display to left. Here each character will be scrolled to left at a time delay of 500 milli seconds.

Program:

```
#include <LiquidCrystal.h>
LiquidCrystal lcd(12, 11, 5, 4, 3, 2); // sets the interfacing
pins (RS,Enable,D4,D5,D6,D7)

void setup()
{
 lcd.begin(16, 2); //initializes 16x2 LCD
  lcd.print ("16x2 LCD MODULE INTERFACING WITH ARDUINO-
UNO");  //text to display
 }

void loop()
{
  lcd.scrollDisplayLeft(); //scrolls display left by two
positions
 delay(500); //sets the speed at which display moves
 }
//end
```

LCD wiTH KeypAd

This project teaches us how to interface a membrane keypad with 12 keys (4 x3) with Arduino board. As we have already discussed about the working of LCD, we shall focus more on keypad. An appropriate diagram for a membrane keypad is shown in figure 10.1. Internally in a keypad, wires run in vertical columns (C0, C1 and C2) and in horizontal rows (R0, R1, R2 and R3). There is a ribbon with 7 wires running from the bottom of the keypad which will be connected to the Arduino digital pins.

Figure 10.1: Membrane keypad 16 key (4x3) diagram

The arrangements of the keys (key-map) are:

- 1 2 3
- 4 5 6
- 7 8 9
- * 0 #

For the above 12-button 4x3 matrix, 7 digital pins of the Arduino board will be used. The first 4 pins will be connected to the ROW wires, while the other 3 pins will be connected to the COLUMN wires. The Arduino pins connected to the COLUMN wires are configured as OUTPUT and are powered one by one in a cycle. The pins with the ROW wire connection are configured as INPUT to monitor whether any key is pressed or not. Each key on the keypad is essentially a switch that connects a row wire to a column wire. When a key is pressed, it makes an electrical connection between the row and column. As long as the pins with the ROW wire connection are LOW, it means no key is pressed.

Components

- Arduino board
- Membrane Keypad (4x3)
- Liquid Crystal Display (16×2)
- Breadboard

Project 10.1: Interfacing 4x3 keypad with Arduino

To start with the project, we shall program the Arduino to check the proper working of the keypad and its connections. As we are already familiar with serial monitor, we shall observe whether we get the same character on the serial monitor when the character on the keypad is pressed.

Explanation:

Arduino 'Keypad.h' library needs to be included in the Arduino sketch to avail the use of inbuilt keypad functions. The library is non-blocking which means you can press and hold the key but the microcontroller in the Arduino will continue processing the rest of your code. The library supports user defined pins and key-maps.

The following program enables us to write the keypad characters on the serial monitor. The program is constructed such that every key we press on the keypad, the

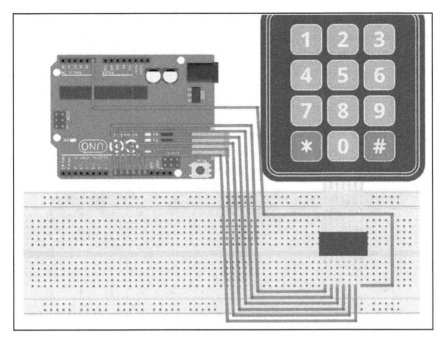

Figure 10.2: 4x3 Keypad with Arduino wiring diagram

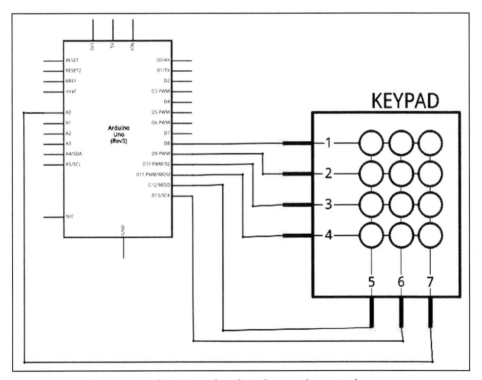

Figure 10.3: 4x3 Keypad with Arduino schematic diagram

corresponding character appears on the serial monitor. The 7 pins of the keypad are wired to Arduino through digital pins '8' to '13'and analog pin A0 (used as digital pin). The function getKey() returns a key value as soon as you press the key. The keymap for the keypad is user defined and can be changed according to the need of the task. An object 'keypad' is declared relating with information about its connection and the size of rows and columns.

Upload the program to Arduino board and open the serial monitor for testing. On the event of the key being pressed the corresponding keypad character is displayed on the serial monitor. The result of testing each key is shown below.

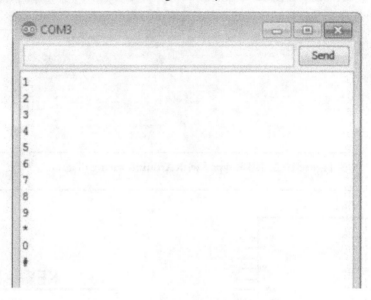

Program:

```
#include <Keypad.h> //include keypad library
const byte ROWS = 4; // set display to four rows
const byte COLS = 3; // set display to three columns
char keys[ROWS][COLS] = { // user defined keypmap
{'1','2','3'},
{'4','5','6'},
{'7','8','9'},
{'*','0','#'}
};
byte rowPins[ROWS] = {8,9,10,11}; //connect to row
R0,R1,R2,R3
byte colPins[COLS] = {12,13,A0}; //connect to column
C0,C1,C2
```

```
Keypad keypad = Keypad( makeKeymap(keys), rowPins, colPins,
ROWS, COLS );

void setup()
{
Serial.begin(9600); //start serial communication between
Arduino and computer
}

void loop(){
char key = keypad.getKey(); //returns the keypad character
when pressed
if (key != NO_KEY) //if key is pressed
{
Serial.println(key); //print the character on the serial
monitor
}
}
//end
```

Project 10.2: Interfacing 4x3 Keypad and LCD together with Arduino

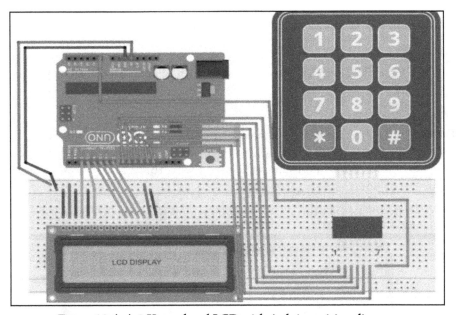

Figure 10.4: 4x3 Keypad and LCD with Arduino wiring diagram

Next in this project we'll use a LCD to display the keypad characters. This requires a few modifications to the earlier sketch. We also need to use the functions from the LCD library which are already discussed in Project 9.1.

Arduino digital pins 2 to 7 are used for LCD connections and pins 8 to 13 and analog pin A0 is used for keypad connection.

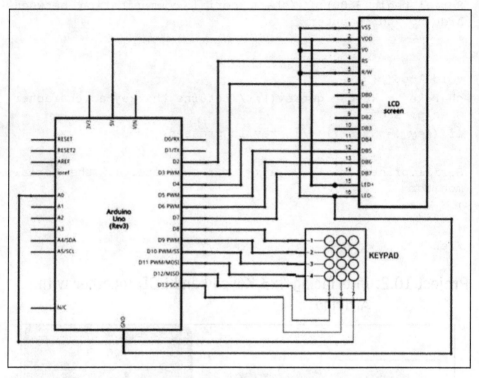

Figure 10.5: 4x3 Keypad and LCD with Arduino schematic diagram

Explanation:

The sketch displays the keypad character on a LCD as and when any key on the keypad is pressed. The key-map in the sketch can be changed as required. Also the sketch can be used for interfacing 4x4 keypad with 16 keys by only increasing the number of columns.

The character pressed on the keypad appears on the LCD display. The figures below show the testing result of each key.

Program:

```
#include <Keypad.h> //include keypad library
#include <LiquidCrystal.h> //include LCD library

LiquidCrystal lcd(2, 3, 4, 5, 6, 7); //LCD connections pins
with Arduino

const byte ROWS = 4; // set display to four rows
const byte COLS = 3; // set display to three columns

char keys[ROWS][COLS] = { //key-map for 4x3 keypad
{'1','2','3'},
{'4','5','6'},
{'7','8','9'},
{'*','0','#'}
};
byte rowPins[ROWS] = {8,9,10,11};    //connect to row
R0,R1,R2,R3
byte colPins[COLS] = {12,13,A0}; //connect to column
C0,C1,C2

Keypad keypad = Keypad( makeKeymap(keys), rowPins, colPins,
ROWS, COLS );

void setup()
{
Serial.begin(9600); //start serial communication between
Arduino and computer
lcd.begin(16, 2);
}

void loop(){
char key = keypad.getKey();

if (key != NO_KEY)
{
  lcd.print(key);      //print the character on the serial
monitor
}
}
//end
```

Project 10.3: Basic Keypad lock system with Arduino

Further let us discuss on creating a basic keypad lock system. The setup is similar to the earlier project. The sketch holds the password which can be changed by the programmer before uploading the sketch to the Arduino board.

Explanation:

The following sketch asks for the user to enter a password. The sketch stores predefined password '123#'. Here '#' is used as the terminating character and every time the user enters '#' the password entered is compared with the predefined one. The password entered by the user is stored in a string variable 'input'.

On comparing, if the password entered is correct then 'CORRECT PASWORD' will be displayed on the LCD. On such an occasion, the user can also actuate a motor or LED based on the need of the project.

And, if the password entered is incorrect then 'TRY AGAIN' will be displayed.

The sketch again waits for the password to be entered after 2 seconds. The programmer can further make modifications as required.

Program:

```
#include <Keypad.h>
#include <LiquidCrystal.h>


// initialize the library with the numbers of the interface
pins
LiquidCrystal lcd(2, 3, 4, 5, 6, 7);
```

```
String input; //variable to store the keypad characters
String password="123#"; //set the password

const byte ROWS = 4;
const byte COLS = 3;

char keys[ROWS][COLS] = {
{'1','2','3'},
{'4','5','6'},
{'7','8','9'},
{'*','0','#'}
};
byte rowPins[ROWS] = {8,9,10,11}; //connect to row
R0,R1,R2,R3
byte colPins[COLS] = {12,13,A0}; //connect to column
C0,C1,C2

Keypad keypad = Keypad( makeKeymap(keys), rowPins, colPins,
ROWS, COLS );

void setup()
{
lcd.begin(16, 2);
reset(); //calling reset function to start over
}

void loop()
{
char key = keypad.getKey(); //get the keypad character

if (key != NO_KEY)
{
  input=input+key;//store the keypad character
  lcd.print('*');
  if(key=='#')
  {
  if(input==password) //if the password entered is correct
```

```
{
lcd.setCursor(0, 1);
lcd.print("CORRECT PASSWORD");
}
else //if the password entered is incorrect
{
lcd.setCursor(0, 1);
lcd.print("TRY AGAIN");
}
delay(2000);
input="";
reset();
}
}
}

void reset()
{
 lcd.clear();
 lcd.print("Enter Password");
 lcd.setCursor(0, 1);
}
//end
```

h a p t e r   Eleven

Dot Matrix Display

Light emitting diodes arranged in a form of matrix constitute a dot matrix display. Dot matrix displays are used for displaying full range of alphanumeric characters and simple graphics when arranged in panels. Everyone must have encountered dot matrix displays in public places displaying advertisements and information. We will discuss about the working of monochrome (red colour) 8x8 LED dot matrix and its interfacing with Arduino for displaying alphanumeric characters.

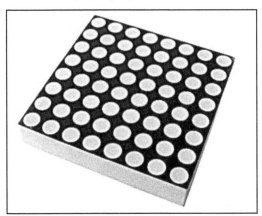

Figure 11.1: An 8x8 dot matrix display

A 8x8 matrix of LED would require 64-I/O pins, one for each pixel for complete control. In order to reduce the need of such high number of I/O pins, LED's are arranged in rows and columns. By connecting all the anodes together in rows (R1 to R8) and cathodes in columns (C1 to C8), the number of I/O pins required reduces to 16. Each LED is addressed by its row and column number. As you can see from figure 11.2, when C2 is pulled high and R3 is pulled low, the LED in third row and second column will be turned on.

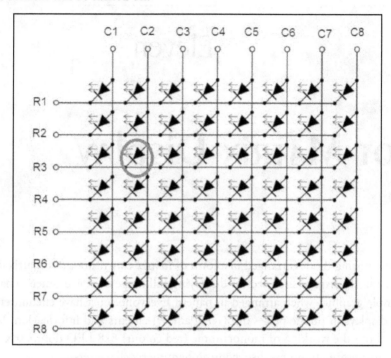

Figure 11.2: Structure of an 8x8 dot matrix display

For displaying still characters on dot matrix display, we use the scanning method to turn ON the required LED's on the first column and then the designated LED's on the next column and so on. The columns are selected by applying forward bias voltage to one column at a time and pulling low the corresponding rows. The process of scanning is fast enough (>40Hz) which makes all the designated LED's appear to be ON at the same time. In other words, the persistence of vision comes into play and we perceive the character to be still. Dot matrix display 1088AS is used in this project which is common cathode type.

The 1088AS is an 8x8 LED dot matrix display. It is available in a package with 16 pins arranged in DIP and its type is common cathode. The figure below illustrates the pin diagram of a 1088AS dot matrix display.

There are many different ways to drive dot matrix display but one of the most popular ways is by using MAX7219 LED driver IC. The MAX7219 are compact, common-cathode display drivers that interface microcontrollers to 8x8 LED matrix displays. Only one external resistor is required to set the segment current for all LEDs. Following table shows the ratings of MAX7219.

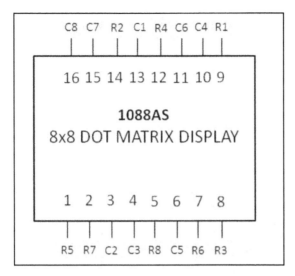

Figure 11.3: 1088AS pin diagram

Table 11.1: MAX7219 Specifications

S.No	Parameter	Value
1.	Power Supply	4.0V ~ 5.5V
2.	Supply current	330mA
3.	Scan Rate	800Hz (Typ)
4.	Clock	10MHz
5.	Logic High Input	3.5V (min)
6.	Logic Low Input	0.4V (max)

MAX7219 are available in 24 DIP package and has wide applications with Bar-Graph Displays, Panel Meters, Industrial Controllers and LED Matrix Displays.

Figure 11.4: MAX7219 LED driver IC

The next figure illustrates the pin configuration of MAX7219.

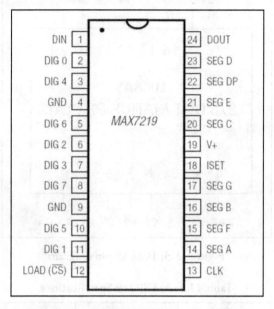

Figure 11.5: MAX7219 pin configuration

Components

- Arduino board
- MAX7219
- Dot matrix display (1088AS)
- Resistance (10kΩ)
- Breadboard

Project 11.1: Displaying Alphanumeric Characters on Dot Matrix Display

An 8x8 dot matrix display is used to display alphanumeric characters. As shown in the figure 11.2, we require 16 digital pins to drive 1088AS dot matrix display. We know that there are only 14 digital pins are available on the Arduino board. The is full filled by using MAX7219 driver IC to interface 8x8 dot matrix display with Arduino.

A convenient three serial interface (SPI) connects MAX7219 and Arduino. The first one is the clock line (CLK) which provides the necessary clock pulses and the second line called data line (DATA) helps in transmitting serial data. The third line is the chip select line (CS) used to activate the LED driver chip. The CS line must be LOW for the driver chip to accept the data and HIGH immediately after the data has been completely delivered. 16 bit serial data at DIN pin of the driver chip MAX7219 is propagated to the DOUT pin through the shift registers after 16.5 clock cycles. The supply to the driver chip is provided from the 5V and GND terminal of Arduino. Only three wires are required to connect Arduino and MAX 7219.

Table 11.2: Arduino and MAX7219 connections

Arduino Pins	MAX 7219 Pins
12	1
11	13
10	12

The 16 output lines from MAX7219 drives 64 individual LED's of 8x8 dot matrix display. Therefore there are 16 connections to made between the LED matrix 1088AS and the LED driver chip MAX 7219. Follow the connection pattern mentioned in table below for proper interfacing of 1088AS and MAX7219.

Table 11.3: 1088AS and MAX7219 interfacing

1088AS pins		MAX7219 pins	
Pin Name	Pin No	Pin Name	Pin No
R1	9	DIG 0	2
R2	14	DIG 1	11
R3	8	DIG 2	6
R4	12	DIG 3	7
R5	1	DIG 4	3
R6	7	DIG 5	10
R7	2	DIG 6	5
R8	5	DIG 7	8
C1	13	SEG DP	22
C2	3	SEG A	14
C3	4	SEG B	16
C4	10	SEG C	20
C5	6	SEG D	23
C6	11	SEG E	21
C7	15	SEG F	15
C8	16	SEG G	17

The figure below illustrates the circuit diagram required to get the dot matrix display working. A resistance of 10kΩ is used to control the current through each column of the dot matrix display within limits i.e. less than 40mA. Remember to interconnect the Arduino 5V and GND terminal with the MAX 7219 pins 19 and 4 respectively for power supply.

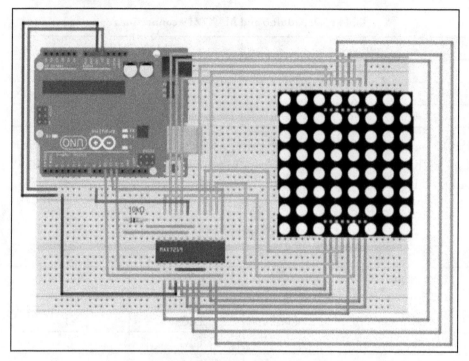

Figure 11.6: Arduino and 1088AS interfacing with MAX 7219 wiring diagram

Explanation:

Firstly in the program we need to include the library 'LedControl.h' so that we can use the inbuilt functions which make the program simple and easy to understand. The next line sets up an instance to control the display patterns.

LedControl lc=LedControl(DIN,CLK,CS,0);

Pin 12, 11 and 10 of Arduino is connected to the DIN, CLK, and LOAD pin of the Max7219 IC. The fourth parameter indicates the number of cascaded LED driver ICs.

For displaying any character, you need to obtain the 8 byte hexadecimal code for that particular character. We can do the same manually or we can take the help of software called 'PixelToMatrix' which can be downloaded from http://www.educ8s. com/Arduino/LedMatrix.

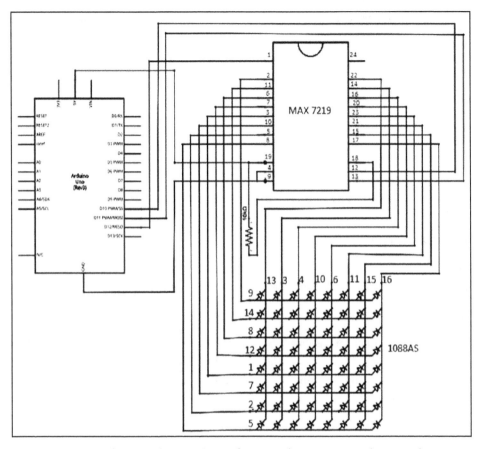

Figure 11.7: Arduino and 1088AS interfacing with MAX 7219 schematic diagram

For instance if we want to display character 'A' in an 8x8 display, the display would look something like this.

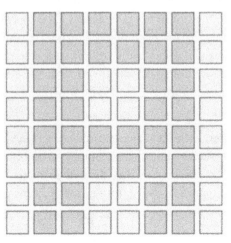

For which the binary code corresponding to each row would be written as:

- 0 1 1 1 1 1 1 0
- 0 1 1 1 1 1 1 0
- 0 1 1 0 0 1 1 0
- 0 1 1 0 0 1 1 0
- 0 1 1 1 1 1 1 0
- 0 1 1 1 1 1 1 0
- 0 1 1 0 0 1 1 0
- 0 1 1 0 0 1 1 0

Binary '1' for the LED which is ON and binary '0' for the LED which is OFF. The hexadecimal equivalent for the above binary code will be as given below.

{0x7E,0x7E,0x66,0x66,0x7E,0x7E,0x66,0x66}

Similarly in the program we have generated 8 byte hexadecimal codes for characters 'A', 'B', 'C', 'D', 'E', '1', '2', '3', '4' and '5'. With proper wiring, the dot matrix display should show the characters one after the other at a delay of one second once the program is uploaded.

The functions inside the setup() controls the display during start up.

```
lc.shutdown(0,false);
lc.setIntensity(0,8);
```

The 'shutdown' function turns all the LED's ON and active. If we set the parameter as 'true', the LEDs will stay OFF even though the data is sent from driver MAX 7219. This can be used when we want to turn the display OFF to avoid unwanted displays. The second line controls the intensity of the dot matrix display. The intensity can be controlled by altering the value of the second parameter from 0 to 15. The first parameter for both the functions indicates the number of MAX 7219 ICs connected in parallel. This allows us to turn ON and OFF individual displays and also control their intensity of display.

Inside the loop function, each character is displayed on the 8x8 dot matrix display board at an interval of one second. This is done by setting the LEDs on each row at a time. Similarly one can display any user defined character by only generating the corresponding hexadecimal code. The output of the project would look similar to the one shown below.

Program:

```
#include <LedControl.h>

int DIN = 12;
int CS = 10;
int CLK = 11;
LedControl lc=LedControl(DIN,CLK,CS,0);
byte a[8]= {0x7E,0x7E,0x66,0x66,0x7E,0x7E,0x66,0x66};
//hexadecimal code for character 'A'
byte b[8]= {0x7E,0x7E,0x66,0x7E,0x7E,0x66,0x7E,0x7E};
//hexadecimal code for character 'B'
byte c[8]= {0x7E,0x7E,0x60,0x60,0x60,0x60,0x7E,0x7E};
//hexadecimal code for character 'C'
byte d[8]= {0x78,0x7C,0x66,0x66,0x66,0x66,0x7C,0x78};
//hexadecimal code for character 'D'
byte e[8]= {0x7C,0x7C,0x60,0x7C,0x7C,0x60,0x7C,0x7C};
//hexadecimal code for character 'E'

byte one[8]= {0x78,0x78,0x58,0x18,0x18,0x18,0x7E,0x7E};
      //hexadecimal code for character '1'
byte two[8]= {0x3C,0x3C,0x2C,0x0C,0x3C,0x30,0x3C,0x3C};
      //hexadecimal code for character '2'
byte three[8]= {0x3E,0x3E,0x06,0x1E,0x1E,0x06,0x3E,0x3E};
      //hexadecimal code for character '3'
```

```
byte four[8]= {0x6C,0x6C,0x6C,0x7C,0x7C,0x0C,0x0C,0x0C};
     //hexadecimal code for character '4'
byte five[8]= {0x7C,0x7C,0x40,0x7C,0x7C,0x0C,0x7C,0x7C};
     //hexadecimal code for character '5'


void setup(){
  lc.shutdown(0,false);   //The MAX72XX is in power-saving
mode on start up
  lc.setIntensity(0,8); // Set the brightness
lc.clearDisplay(0);     // Clear the display
}


void loop()
{
 printByte(a);                    //print character 'A'
 delay(1000);
 printByte(b);                    //print character 'B'
 delay(1000);
 printByte(c);                    //print character 'C'
 delay(1000);
 printByte(d);                    //print character 'D'
 delay(1000);
 printByte(e);                    //print character 'E'
 delay(1000);
 printByte(one);                  //print character '1'
 delay(1000);
 printByte(two);                  //print character '2'
 delay(1000);
 printByte(three);                //print character '3'
 delay(1000);
 printByte(four);                 //print character '4'
 delay(1000);
 printByte(five);                 //print character '5'
 delay(1000);
}
void printByte(byte character []) // print the character
{
```

```
 int i = 0;
 for(i=0;i<8;i++)
 {
 lc.setRow(0,i,character[i]);          //set each row at
a time
 }
}

//end
```

C hapter Twelve

7 Seqment Display

In this project we want to use a 7 segment display with 4543 BCD to 7 Segment Driver to display decimal digits. Moreover, the 7 segment displays can be used to display both decimal and hexadecimal digits. Seven-segment displays are widely used in digital clocks, electronic meters, and other electronic devices for displaying numerical information. 7 segment modules are made up of 8 LEDs, where an additional 8th LED is sometimes used to allow the indication of a decimal point (DP). All these seven individually LED pins are labeled from 'a' through to 'g', and the other ends of the LED's are connected together and wired to form a common pin.

Figure 12.1: A typical 7-segment display

Components

- Arduino board
- 7 Segment Display

- HEF 4543

- Resistances (1kΩ)

- Transistor 2N2222

- Breadboard

Project 12.1: Display of Bumeric Characters using 7 Segment Display

There are two important types of 7-segment LED display depending on the common pin (COM) connection. In a common cathode display, the cathodes of all the LEDs are joined together and the individual segments are illuminated by HIGH voltages. In a common anode display, the anodes of all the LEDs are joined together and the individual segments are illuminated by connecting to a LOW voltage.

In order to generate the required character pattern, the corresponding pins of the LED segment needs to be forward biased. This then allows us to display each of the ten decimal digits 0 through to 9 on the same 7-segment display. If we take an example of common cathode type 7 segment display, we need to connect the common pin (COM) to the ground terminal of the supply and the segments from 'a' to 'g' are accordingly set HIGH via a current limiting resistor to display a particular character. The value of the limiting resistor effects the illumination of the LED segments.

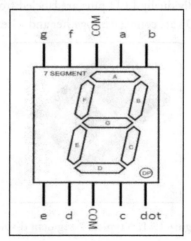

Figure 12.2: Pin out diagram of 7-segment display

HEF 4543 is a 7 segment decoder driver made up of n-p-n transistors and therefore used for driving common cathode LED displays. HEF 4543 makes possible to drive the 7 segment delay with only four digital pins of the Arduino board.

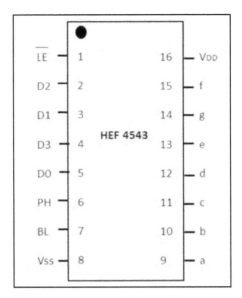

Figure 12.3: HEF 4543 pin configuration

The 4543 takes a four-bit BCD input (D0, D1, D2 and D3) on pins 5, 3, 2, and 4 respectively. Binary Coded Decimal (BCD) means that each decimal digit is individually coded in binary. For example the decimal number '9' is 1001 in BCD. These BCD input to the driver 4543 determines the state of the outputs ('a' to 'g').

When the 4543 is set up correctly, the outputs follow this truth table:

Table 12.1: Functional description of HEF 4543

BCD inputs				segment outputs							Display
D3	D2	D1	D0	a	b	c	d	e	f	g	
0	0	0	0	1	1	1	1	1	1	0	0
0	0	0	1	0	1	1	0	0	0	0	1
0	0	1	0	1	1	0	1	1	0	1	2
0	0	1	1	1	1	1	1	0	0	0	3
0	1	0	0	0	1	1	0	0	1	1	4
0	1	0	1	1	0	1	1	0	1	1	5
0	1	1	0	0	0	1	1	1	1	1	6
0	1	1	1	1	1	1	0	0	0	0	7
1	0	0	0	1	1	1	1	1	1	1	8
1	0	0	1	1	1	1	0	1	1	1	9

The HEF 4543 is a BCD to 7-segment latch/decoder/driver along with an active high phase (PH), active high blanking input (BL), and active low latch enable ($\overline{LE}$) inputs are used to reverse the function table phase, blank the display and store a BCD code respectively. Phase (PH) input enables driving of both common anode and common cathode 7 segment displays.

Table 12.2: Pin description of HEF 4543

Sl.No.	Pin	Symbol	Description
1.	16	Vdd	Supply Voltage
2.	8	Vss	Ground
3.	5, 3, 2, 4	D0, D1, D2, D3	BCD data Input
4.	9, 10, 11, 12, 13, 14, 15	a,b,c,d,e,f,g	Output
5.	1	$\overline{LE}$	Latch Enable
6.	6	PH	Phase Input
7.	7	BL	Blanking Input

When $\overline{LE}$ is HIGH and BL is LOW, the state of the outputs ('a' to 'g') is determined by the data on driver inputs D0 to D3. In other words, the outputs follow the logic states of the BCD inputs and the 7-segment outputs change accordingly. When $\overline{LE}$ goes LOW, the last data present on D0 to D3 is stored in the latches and the driver outputs remain unchanged.

When PH is low, the outputs in the segment 'a' to 'g' will be according to the table 12.1 as shown above which is suitable for driving common cathode LED segments as shown in figure 12.4 (a). In order to drive common anode LED segments, the Phase (PH) input is set HIGH and the driver outputs will be inversed. With Phase (PH) LOW, a HIGH on BL forces all segment outputs LOW for any combination of binary input to the driver.

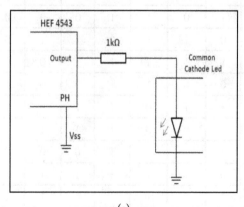

(a)

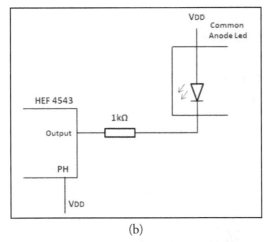

(b)

Figure 12.4: HEF 4543 connection to LED segment for
(a) Common Cathode (b) Common Anode

The 4543 driver has a built-in 4-bit latch (a set of flip-flops) that can permanently retain a binary-coded decimal (BCD) input. When the latch-enable ($\overline{LE}$) pin 1 is HIGH and the blanking input (BL) and phase input (PH) pins are low, the 7 segment display is a base-ten representation of the 4-bit BCD number applied to pins 5, 3, 2 and 4.

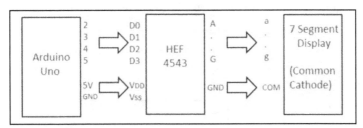

Figure 12.5: Interconnection block diagram for 7 segment display

Explanation:

The aim of the project is to drive a 7 segment display using a HEF 4543 LED driver IC. There are other drivers such as HEF 4511, CD 4511, CD 4543, shift register 74HC595 and MAX 7219 which can also be used to drive a 7 segment LED. With the help of these driver ICs it is possible to drive a 7 segment display using only four digital pins of Arduino board i.e. (2, 3, 4 and 5). These four digital pins are connected to the four inputs (D0, D1, D2 and D3) of HEF 4543. The BCD to 7 segment decoder inside HEF 4543 converts the BCD input to seven outputs to drive the 7 segment display. The circuit runs on the 5V supply from the Arduino board. The GND terminal of Arduino and GND of HEF 4543 forms a common node. Common cathode type display is used and therefore the COM pin of the display

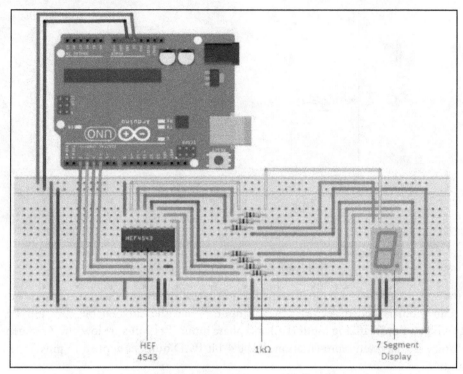

Figure 12.6: HEF 4543 driven 7 Segment display circuit diagram

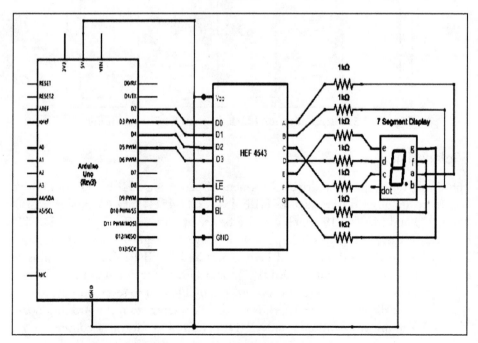

Figure 12.7: HEF 4543 driven 7 Segment display schematic diagram

must be connected to the common GND terminal. Seven 1 kilo ohm resistors are used as current limiters for the 7 segment display. The latch-enable ($\overline{LE}$) pin is connected to 5V so that the display updates itself every time the BCD input changes.

The program below displays numeric characters from '0' to '9' at an interval of one second. For displaying each character, the corresponding BCD is written on the D0, D1, D2 and D3 pins of HEF 4543 through Arduino digital pins 2, 3, 4 and 5. Separate functions for each numeric character are created and are called from the loop function whenever the character needs to be displayed.

Program:

```
int D0=2;    // Sets Digital pin 2 as D0 on 4543
int D1=3;    // Sets Digital pin 3 as D1 on 4543
int D2=4;    // Sets Digital pin 4 as D2 on 4543
int D3=5;    // Sets Digital pin 5 as D3 on 4543

void setup() {
// initialize the digital pin as an output.
 pinMode(D0, OUTPUT);
 pinMode(D1, OUTPUT);
 pinMode(D2, OUTPUT);
 pinMode(D3, OUTPUT);
}

void loop()
{

  call_0(); //calls function call_0 to display decimal
character '0'
 delay(1000);
 call_1(); //calls function call_1 to display decimal
character '1'
 delay(1000);
 call_2(); //calls function call_2 to display decimal
character '2'
 delay(1000);
 call_3(); //calls function call_3 to display decimal
character '3'
 delay(1000);
 call_4(); //calls function call_4 to display decimal
character '4'
```

```
 delay(1000);
 call_5(); //calls  function  call_5  to  display  decimal
character '5'
 delay(1000);
 call_6(); //calls  function  call_6  to  display  decimal
character '6'
 delay(1000);
 call_7(); //calls  function  call_7  to  display  decimal
character '7'
 delay(1000);
 call_8(); //calls  function  call_8  to  display  decimal
character '8'
 delay(1000);
 call_9(); //calls  function  call_9  to  display  decimal
character '9'
 delay(1000);
 }

void call_0()     //function for displaying character '0'
{
 digitalWrite(2, LOW); // Sets D0 as low
 digitalWrite(3, LOW); // Sets D1 as low
 digitalWrite(4, LOW); // Sets D2 as low
 digitalWrite(5, LOW); // Sets D3 as low
}
void call_1()     //function for displaying character '1'
{
 digitalWrite(2, HIGH);
 digitalWrite(3, LOW);
 digitalWrite(4, LOW);
 digitalWrite(5, LOW);
}
void call_2()     //function for displaying character '2'
{
 digitalWrite(2, LOW);
 digitalWrite(3, HIGH);
 digitalWrite(4, LOW);
 digitalWrite(5, LOW);
}
```

```
void call_3()      //function for displaying character '3'
{
 digitalWrite(2, HIGH);
 digitalWrite(3, HIGH);
 digitalWrite(4, LOW);
 digitalWrite(5, LOW);
}
void call_4()      //function for displaying character '4'
{
 digitalWrite(2, LOW);
 digitalWrite(3, LOW);
 digitalWrite(4, HIGH);
 digitalWrite(5, LOW);
}
void call_5()      //function for displaying character '5'
{
 digitalWrite(2, HIGH);
 digitalWrite(3, LOW);
 digitalWrite(4, HIGH);
 digitalWrite(5, LOW);
}
 void call_6()     //function for displaying character '6'
 {
 digitalWrite(2, LOW);
 digitalWrite(3, HIGH);
 digitalWrite(4, HIGH);
 digitalWrite(5, LOW);
 }
 void call_7()     //function for displaying character '7'
 {
 digitalWrite(2, HIGH);
 digitalWrite(3, HIGH);
 digitalWrite(4, HIGH);
 digitalWrite(5, LOW);
 }
 void call_8()     //function for displaying character '8'
 {
 digitalWrite(2, LOW);
 digitalWrite(3, LOW);
```

```
digitalWrite(4, LOW);
digitalWrite(5, HIGH);
}
void call_9()    //function for displaying character '9'
{
digitalWrite(2, HIGH);
digitalWrite(3, LOW);
digitalWrite(4, LOW);
digitalWrite(5, HIGH);
}
//end
```

Project 12.2: Display of Numeric Characters using two 7 Segment Displays and one Decoder

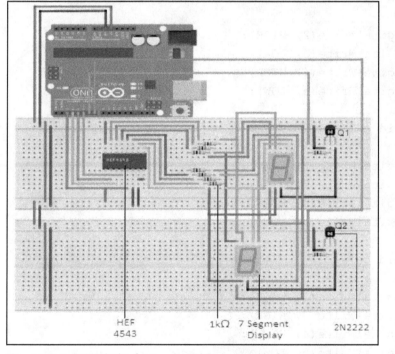

Figure 12.8: HEF 4543 driving two 7 Segment displays circuit diagram

Our next aim is to display two numeric characters at a time using two 7 segment displays but only one HEF 4543 driver. The terminal connection to the second segment display is tapped after the seven 1kΩ resistance of the first segment display. Two n-p-n transistors Q1 and Q2 are also associated with the segment displays and are controlled from digital pins 6 and 7 of the Arduino board respectively. When digital pin 6 is HIGH and Q1 is turned ON. This connects the COM pin of 7 segment display 1 to GND and the numeric character shows up in segment display 1. Similarly when digital pin 7 is set HIGH, Q2 is turned ON and 7 segment display 2 shows up the numeric character.

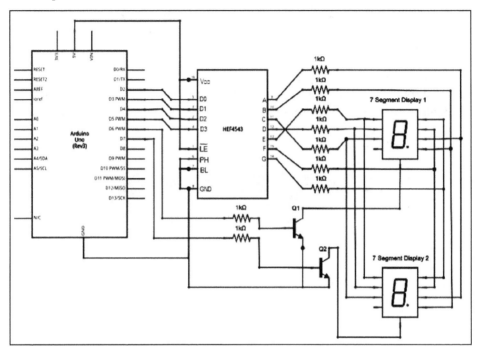

Figure 12.9: HEF 4543 driving two 7 Segment displays schematic diagram

Explanation:

In the second part of this project, we will discuss how to control two 7 segment displays using a single IC HEF 4543. This can be achieved by controlling two NPN transistors (2N2222) through Arduino Uno board. As the data pins are multiplexed, the segment displays needs to be turned on and off alternately. The segment display is selected by appropriately turning on the corresponding transistor. The time delay between the selections of the segment display is suggested to be kept as small as possible in milli seconds. Human eye is unable to notice such a small difference in time and appears to us as both the segment displays are constantly on.

The turning ON and OFF are controlled by the digital pins 6 and 7 of Arduino. These pins are connected to the base of the transistor. Whenever digital pin 6 is set HIGH, the corresponding transistor turns on and thereby the COM terminal of the '7 segment display 1' gets connected to GND. The current binary data on the input data lines of HEF 4543 is played on the '7 segment display 1'.

Similarly to display any character on '7 segment display 2', Arduino digital pin 7 is made HIGH and digital pin 6 LOW. Both the digital pins should never be HIGH at the same time, if so then the same character will be displayed on both the segments simultaneously. The ones digit is obtained by finding the remainder of the two digit decimal number when divided by decimal '10'. Tens digit is obtained by simply dividing the two digit decimal number by 10. '7 segment display 1' is used to display the tens digit and '7 segment display 2' displays the ones digit.

The program takes the two digit input from the user. The digit entered by the user will be displayed on the 7 segment displays. After uploading the program, to enter the digits open the serial monitor of the Arduino IDE by clicking on the icon shown.

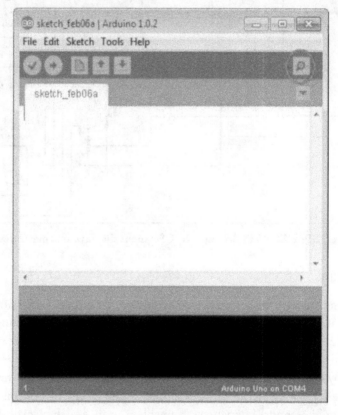

This opens up the serial monitor. Enter the desired two digit value and click on the SEND button. The corresponding numeric characters will be shown up in the two segment displays.

In the same way we can add on more segment displays by turning on individual 7 segment displays with the help of transistors. Other transistors like BC 547, 2N3906 etc. can also be used for the switching purpose. This method of alternatingly turning on each segment display reduces the output current drawn from the Arduino board in case no external battery supply is used because at any instant only one segment display draws current from Arduino board.

Program:

```
int D0=2;    // Sets Digital pin 2 as D0 on 4543
int D1=3;    // Sets Digital pin 3 as D1 on 4543
int D2=4;    // Sets Digital pin 4 as D2 on 4543
int D3=5;    // Sets Digital pin 5 as D3 on 4543
String data="";
int value;

void setup()
{
Serial.begin(9600);
// initialize the digital pin as an output.
pinMode(6, OUTPUT);
pinMode(7, OUTPUT);
```

```
pinMode(D0, OUTPUT);
pinMode(D1, OUTPUT);
pinMode(D2, OUTPUT);
pinMode(D3, OUTPUT);
}


void loop()
{
while(Serial.available()>0) //run the loop if data is in
the serial buffer
{
char c = Serial.read(); //read the serial data
data=data+c; //append the characters to string 'data'
value= data.toInt(); //converts string 'data' to integer 'value'
}
int ones = value%10; //get the ones digit
digitalWrite(6, LOW); //turn off segment display 1
digitalWrite(7, HIGH); //turn on segment display 2
select(ones); //call the function to select and display the
digit
delay(10); //pause for display
int tens = value/10; //get the tens digit
digitalWrite(6, HIGH); //turn on segment display 1
digitalWrite(7, LOW); //turn off segment display 2
select(tens); // call the function to select and display the
digit
delay(10); //pause for display
data=""; //reinitialise data to null character
}
void select(int number)
{
if(number==0)
call_0(); //calls function call_0 to display decimal character '0'
else if(number==1)
call_1();//calls function call_1 to display decimal character '1'
else if(number==2)
call_2();//calls function call_2 to display decimal character '2'
else if(number==3)
```

```
call_3(); //calls function call_3 to display decimal character '3'
else if(number==4)
call_4(); //calls function call_4 to display decimal character '4'
else if(number==5)
call_5(); //calls function call_5 to display decimal character '5'
else if(number==6)
call_6(); //calls function call_6 to display decimal character '6'
else if(number==7)
call_7(); //calls function call_7 to display decimal character '7'
else if(number==8)
call_8(); //calls function call_8 to display decimal character '8'
else if(number==9)
call_9(); //calls function call_9 to display decimal character '9'
}

void call_0()
{
digitalWrite(2, LOW);   // Sets D0 as low
digitalWrite(3, LOW);   // Sets D1 as low
digitalWrite(4, LOW);   // Sets D2 as low
digitalWrite(5, LOW);   // Sets D3 as low
}
void call_1()
{
digitalWrite(2, HIGH);
digitalWrite(3, LOW);
digitalWrite(4, LOW);
digitalWrite(5, LOW);
}
void call_2()
{
digitalWrite(2, LOW);
digitalWrite(3, HIGH);
digitalWrite(4, LOW);
digitalWrite(5, LOW);
}
void call_3()
{
```

```
digitalWrite(2, HIGH);
digitalWrite(3, HIGH);
digitalWrite(4, LOW);
digitalWrite(5, LOW);
}
void call_4()
{
digitalWrite(2, LOW);
digitalWrite(3, LOW);
digitalWrite(4, HIGH);
digitalWrite(5, LOW);
}
void call_5()
{
digitalWrite(2, HIGH);
digitalWrite(3, LOW);
digitalWrite(4, HIGH);
digitalWrite(5, LOW);
}
void call_6()
{
digitalWrite(2, LOW);
digitalWrite(3, HIGH);
digitalWrite(4, HIGH);
digitalWrite(5, LOW);
}
void call_7()
{
digitalWrite(2, HIGH);
digitalWrite(3, HIGH);
digitalWrite(4, HIGH);
digitalWrite(5, LOW);
}
void call_8()
{
digitalWrite(2, LOW);
digitalWrite(3, LOW);
digitalWrite(4, LOW);
```

```
digitalWrite(5, HIGH);
}
void call_9()
{
digitalWrite(2, HIGH);
digitalWrite(3, LOW);
digitalWrite(4, LOW);
digitalWrite(5, HIGH);
}
//end
```

Project 12.3: Display of Numeric Characters using Two 7 Segment Displays and two Decoders

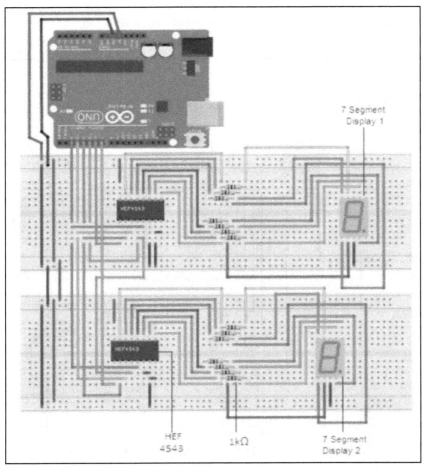

Figure 12.10: Two HEF 4543 driving two 7 Segment displays wiring diagram

The disadvantage of the above method is that the two segment displays needs to constantly switched on and off to display two numbers constantly. This can be avoided with the help of latch enable ($\overline{LE}$) pin of HEF 4543 which is active low. As discussed earlier, the 4543 driver has a built-in 4-bit latch (a set of flip-flops) that can permanently retain a binary-coded decimal (BCD) input. When the latch enable ($\overline{LE}$) is LOW, the 4 bit binary data is latched with the corresponding base ten output. This output will be retained at the pins 'a' to 'g' of HEF 4543. Now if latch enable ($\overline{LE}$) is set HIGH, the 7 segment display is a base-ten representation of the 4-bit BCD number applied to pins 5, 3, 2 and 4. As long as ($\overline{LE}$) is set HIGH, the output of HEF 4543 changes with the change in its 4 bit BCD input.

Two HEF 4543 BCD to 7 segment decoder is used to drive two 7 segment displays. This method is very helpful in applications such as digital clock, electronic meters, and calculators where the character needs to be displayed and kept on hold. Here the 4 bit binary input to the two 4543 decoders is multiplexed unlike the output pins in the earlier project. A total of 6 digital pins of Arduino board are used, 4 output data pins and two digital pins to control the latch enable pins of two 4543 decoder.

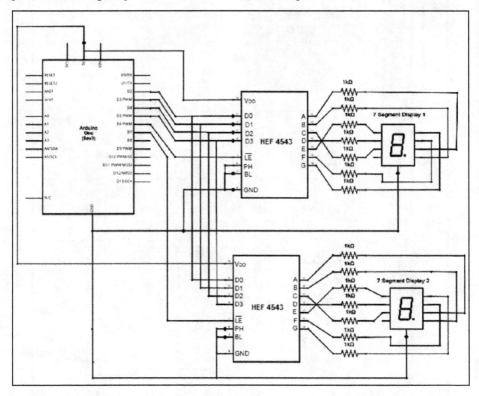

Figure 12.11: Two HEF 4543 driving two 7 Segment displays schematic diagram

Explanation:

The program below counts from decimal 0 to 99 and simultaneously displays the digits on the two segment displays with each decimal number being displayed for half a second. Digital pin 6 and 7 of Arduino are connected to the latch enable (LE) of 4543 decoder. The ones digit is obtained by finding the remainder of the two digit decimal number when divided by decimal '10'. Tens digit is obtained by simply dividing the two digit decimal number by 10. We are using bitwise operators to get the corresponding boolean value for each bit of a decimal number. This is done by using the statement *'boolean z=(v&(1<<b)?HIGH:LOW)'*. Here 'v' stores the binary equivalent of the data to be displayed and 'b' holds the bit position for which the boolean value needs to be calculated. The symbol '<<' denotes left shift operator. This operator causes the bits in the left operand to be shifted left by the number of positions specified by the right operand. For example:

```
int a = 5;   // binary:00101
int b = a << 2;   // binary: 10100
```

Therefore in the statement *'boolean z=(v&(1<<b)?HIGH:LOW)', the sub-statement '(1<<b)'* shifts the high bit '1' to left according to the value of 'b'. The sub-statement *'(v&(1<<b)',* performs AND operation between *'v'* and *'(1<<b)'* at each bit position. The result of the AND operation is a single bit and if it is high i.e. '1' then 'z' will be assigned boolean value 'HIGH' and if the AND operation yields '0' then 'z' will be updated with boolean value 'LOW'.

Program:

```
int D0=2;    // Sets Digital pin 2 as D0 on 4543
int D1=3;    // Sets Digital pin 3 as D1 on 4543
int D2=4;    // Sets Digital pin 4 as D2 on 4543
int D3=5;    // Sets Digital pin 5 as D3 on 4543

int tens;    //integer to store tens digit
int ones;    //integer to store ones digit

// the setup routine runs once when you reset:
void setup()
{
  // initialize the digital pin as an output.
pinMode(6, OUTPUT);
pinMode(7, OUTPUT);
pinMode(D0, OUTPUT);
```

```
pinMode(D1, OUTPUT);
pinMode(D2, OUTPUT);
pinMode(D3, OUTPUT);
}


void loop()
{
for(int i=0;i<=99;i++)//loop to count from '0' to '99'
{
ones = i%10; //get the ones digit
tens = i/10; //get the tens digit
segment_1(); //call function to latch and display in segment 1
segment_2();//call function to latch and display in segment 2
delay(500); //wait for display
}
}


void display_digit(int value)
{
digitalWrite(D0, get_boolean(value,0)); //write the boolean
variable at digital pin D0
digitalWrite(D1, get_boolean (value,1)); //write the boolean
variable at digital pin D1
digitalWrite(D2, get_boolean (value,2)); //write the boolean
variable at digital pin D2
digitalWrite(D3, get_boolean (value,3)); //write the boolean
variable at digital pin D3
}


void segment_1() //function to display tens digit
{
display_digit(tens); //call function to get the 4 bit binary
data
digitalWrite(6, HIGH);
digitalWrite(6, LOW); //switch from HIGH to LOW to latch
the input data
}


void segment_2() //function to display ones digit
```

```
{
display_digit(ones); //call function to get the 4 bit binary
data
digitalWrite(7, HIGH);
digitalWrite(7, LOW); //switch from HIGH to LOW to latch
the input data
}


boolean get_boolean(int v,int b) //function which returns
boolean variable for each bit
{
  boolean z=(v&(1<<b)?HIGH:LOW); //evaluate the boolean
variable for decimal 'v' at 'b' bit position
  return z; //return the boolean variable to the calling
function
}

//end
```

Unipolar Stepper Motor

This chapter introduces us to a new type of motor which rotates in discrete step angles called Stepper Motor. Like any other motor, stepper motor also consists of two primary parts namely stator and rotor. Stator has multiple coils that are organized in groups called "phases". By energizing each phase in sequence, the motor will rotate one step at a time. This step is measured in degrees called step angle. This feature of stepper motor makes it suitable for interfacing and controlling using a microcontroller. There are a wide variety of stepper motors, some of which require very specialized drivers. For our project, we will focus on stepper motors that can be driven with commonly available drivers, some of which we have already covered in the earlier projects. Therefore in this project and the next one, we will learn how to run Unipolar and Bipolar Hybrid stepper motors using simple drivers.

Components

- Arduino board
- Unipolar Stepper Motor (14PM-M201)
- Transistor 2N2222
- ULN2003A
- Diode IN4001
- Resistance (1kΩ)
- Potentiometer (100kΩ)

- LED

- Push Button

- Battery 4.8V

- Breadboard

Following are the basic types of stepper motor:

1. **Variable Reluctance Stepper Motor:** It has wound stator poles but the rotor poles are non-magnetized and made of ferromagnetic material. The rotor has teeth and is designed for small step angle rotation. When the stator coils are energized, the rotor starts moving in forward or reverse direction depending on the switching sequence. The rotor will always try to align itself so as to form a minimum reluctance path and thereby rotates by a step angle.

2. **Permanent Magnet Stepper Motor:** The stator of Permanent Magnet Stepper Motor is also wound as in case of Variable Reluctance Stepper Motor. But the rotor of Permanent Magnet Stepper Motor is made of permanent magnet due to which the direction of rotation depends on the direction of current in the stator poles. The resolution of rotor rotation can be improved by either increasing the number of stator phases or by increasing the number of stator poles.

3. **Hybrid Stepper Motor:** As the name suggests, the Hybrid Stepper Motor combines the characteristics of both Variable Reluctance and Permanent Magnet Stepper Motor. The rotor of Hybrid Stepper Motor is magnetized and also has teeth as in case of Variable Reluctance Stepper Motor. This type of stepper motor finds its application which requires small step angles like 1.8°, 2.5° etc.

4. Hybrid Stepper Motors are further subdivided into Unipolar and Bipolar Stepper Motor based on the direction of the flow of current in the stator winding. Firstly we will study about Unipolar Stepper Motor and Bipolar Stepper Motor and its control will be discussed in chapter 14.

Project 13.1: Unipolar Stepper Motor Control using Transistors

Unipolar Stepper Motor rotates in discrete step angles of 30, 15, 2 and 1.8 degrees with steps per revolution of 12, 24, 180 and 200 respectively. Unlike servo motors, stepper motors can be operated at high degree of accuracy with any feedback mechanism. This project shall discuss about the operation and control of unipolar stepper motors using 2N2222 transistors and ULN2003A. Unipolar stepper motor 14PM-M201 is considered for the project with specifications as listed in the following table.

Table 13.1: Specifications of Unipolar Stepper Motor (14PM-M201)

Sl.No	Parameter	Value
1.	Phase Current	0.4A
2.	Resistance	9Ω
3.	Inductance	4.2mH
4.	Holding torque	5mN-m
5.	Step Angle	1.8 deg
6.	Rated Voltage	6V

Unipolar motors typically have two coils per phase, one for each direction of magnetic field. Unipolar Stepper Motor is generally provided with 5 or 6 wire leads. In case of 6 wire leads, 2 wires 'A COM' and 'B COM' needs to be connected to supply voltage. Only one common wire 'COM' should be powered for Unipolar Stepper Motor with 5 wire leads. A typical 6-wire and 5 wire lead stepper motor schematic diagram is shown in figure 13.1 (a) and (b) respectively. Unipolar Stepper Motor (14PM-M201) with 6 wire lead is used for this project.

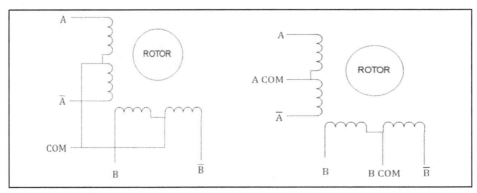

Figure 13.1: Unipolar stepper motor with (a) 6 wire lead and (b) 5 wire lead

The phase connections on the 6 wire leads can be identified either by the colour of the wire or by the pin numbers. Phase 'A COM' and 'B COM' should be connected to the supply voltage and the other phases 'A', 'B', 'Ā' and 'B̄' needs to be sequentially connected to ground terminal to rotate the motor. With this kind of connection the unidirectional current flows through the phase windings and hence the name Unipolar Stepper Motor.

Table 13.2: Pin number with Phase

Phase	A	A COM	Ā	B	B COM	B̄
Colour	Red	Black	Yellow	Blue	White	Orange
Pin No	4	5	6	3	2	1

The sequence in which each phase should be grounded for clockwise rotation is 'A', 'B', 'Ā' and 'B̄' as shown in table 13.3. For counter-clockwise rotation, the phase sequence that needs to be adopted is 'B̄', 'Ā', 'B' and 'A' as shown in table 13.4.

Table 13.3: Unipolar stepper motor switching sequence for Clockwise rotation

Step	A	B	Ā	B̄	A COM B COM
1	—	0	0	0	+
2	0	—	0	0	+
3	0	0	—	0	+
4	0	0	0	—	+

Table 13.4: Unipolar stepper motor switching sequence for Counter-Clockwise rotation

Step	A	B	Ā	B̄	A COM B COM
1	0	0	0	—	+
2	0	0	—	0	+
3	0	—	0	0	+
4	—	0	0	0	+

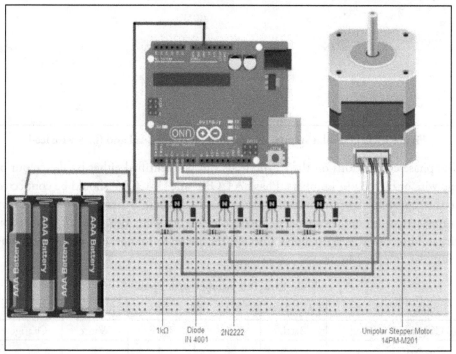

Figure 13.2: Unipolar stepper motor with transistor 2N2222 wiring diagram

In the first section of this project, the switching of the phase sequence is controlled by using an n-p-n transistor 2N2222. N-channel MOSFET IRF 540N can also be used for the switching purpose. The base of each of the four transistors is controlled with the Arduino digital pins.

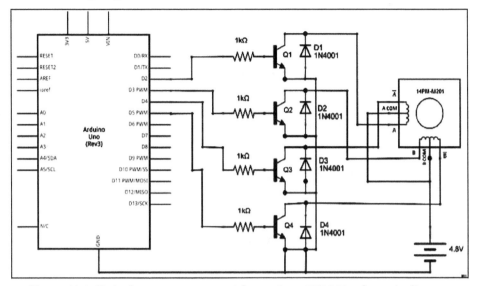

Figure 13.3: Unipolar stepper motor with transistor 2N2222 schematic diagram

Explanation:

The digital pins 2, 3, 4 and 5 of Arduino are connected to the base of the four transistors Q1, Q2, Q3 and Q4 through 1kΩ resistance to limit the base current. When the digital pin 2 is 'HIGH', transistor Q1 is switched on. Phase 'A' connects to ground terminal through transistor Q1 and thereby exciting phase 'A'. Similarly, transistor Q2, Q3 and Q4 control the excitation of phase B', 'A' and 'B' respectively. The program below rotates the stepper motor in clockwise direction by setting the digital pins 2, 3, 4 and 5 high in a sequential manner. A delay of few milli seconds needs to be introduced after every excitation to allow the motor to reach the required position. A diode IN 4001 is placed in anti-parallel across each of the transistors for the protection of the transistor against voltage spikes. The program below runs the stepper motor continuously in clockwise direction.

Program:

```
void setup() {
// initialize the digital pin as an output.
pinMode(2, OUTPUT);
pinMode(3, OUTPUT);
```

```
pinMode(4, OUTPUT);
pinMode(5, OUTPUT);

}
void loop()
{
digitalWrite(2, HIGH); //phase A on
delay(100);
digitalWrite(2, LOW);  //phase A off

digitalWrite(3, HIGH); //phase B on
delay(100);
digitalWrite(3, LOW);  //phase B off

digitalWrite(4, HIGH); //phase on
delay(100);
digitalWrite(4, LOW);  //phase off

digitalWrite(5, HIGH); //phase on
delay(100);
digitalWrite(5, LOW);  //phase off
}
//end
```

Project 13.2: Unipolar Stepper motor Direction Control

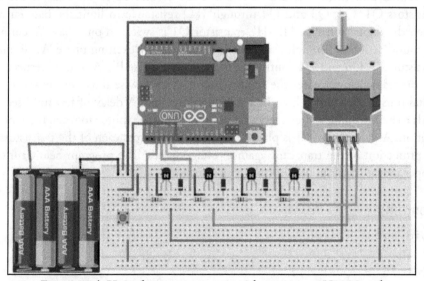

Figure 13.4: Unipolar stepper motor with transistor 2N2222 and push button wiring diagram

In the second portion of this project, a push button is used to control the direction of rotation of the stepper motor. The push button is acting as a switch to set digital pin 6 of Arduino board to +5V (HIGH) or 0V (LOW). When the push button is pressed, digital pin 6 is set HIGH and when the push button is released, digital pin 6 is set back to LOW.

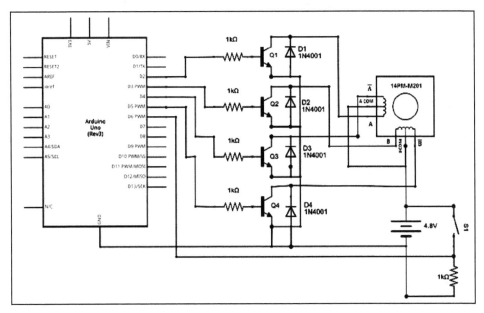

Figure 13.5: Unipolar stepper motor with transistor 2N2222 and push button schematic diagram

Explanation:

In this example, the Unipolar Stepper Motor rotates in clockwise direction when the push button is pressed. As soon as the push button is released, the motor starts running in counter clockwise direction.

Program:

```
void setup()
{
// initialize the digital pin as an output.
pinMode(2, OUTPUT);
pinMode(3, OUTPUT);
pinMode(4, OUTPUT);
pinMode(5, OUTPUT);
pinMode(6, INPUT);
```

```
}

void loop()
{

if(digitalRead(6)==HIGH)
{
//Clockwise rotation
digitalWrite(2, HIGH); //phase A on
delay(100);
digitalWrite(2, LOW);        //phase A off

digitalWrite(3, HIGH); //phase B on
delay(100);
digitalWrite(3, LOW);        //phase B off

digitalWrite(4, HIGH);   //phase on
delay(100);
digitalWrite(4, LOW);        //phase off

digitalWrite(5, HIGH); //phase on
delay(100);
digitalWrite(5, LOW);        //phase off
}

if(digitalRead(6)==LOW)
{
//Counter Clockwise rotation
digitalWrite(5, HIGH); //phase on
delay(100);
digitalWrite(5, LOW);        //phase off

digitalWrite(4, HIGH); //phase on
delay(100);
digitalWrite(4, LOW);        //phase off

digitalWrite(3, HIGH); //phase B on
delay(100);
digitalWrite(3, LOW);        //phase B off
```

```
digitalWrite(2, HIGH); //phase A on
delay(100);
digitalWrite(2, LOW);          //phase A off
}


}
//end
```

Project 13.3: Unipolar stepper motor control using ULN2003A

In the next section, we will explore ULN2003A IC which consists of seven n-p-n Darlington Transistor array for driving Unipolar Stepper Motor. The seven Darlington pair is provided with open collector and common emitters. A Darlington is an arrangement of two bipolar transistors in order to increase the current gain than each transistor taken separately. Each Darlington pair is rated at 500mA collector current.

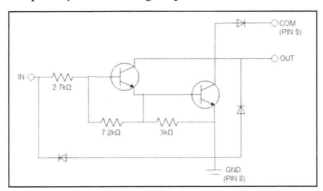

Figure 13.6: Single Darlington pair schematic diagram

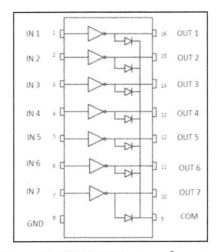

Figure 13.7:ULN2003A pin configuration

The ULN2003A has a 2.7K ohm series base resistor for each Darlington pair for operation directly with TTL or 5-V CMOS devices. These ICs are used as relay drivers as well as to drive a wide range of loads, display drivers etc. This IC is also normally used for driving Stepper Motors. Suppression diodes are provided in the package for driving inductive loads. The figure below shows the pin configuration of ULN2003A.

Now we shall regulate the speed of Unipolar Stepper Motor using ULN2003A driver IC. The digital pins 2, 3, 4 and 5 is directly connected to the input pins IN1, IN2, IN3 and IN4 of ULN2003A which controls the motion of stepper motor. On the event of HIGH signal at digital pin 2, the first Darlington pair turns on thereby causing phase A to get excited and so on. The circuit also consists of four LEDs with resistors to observe the sequential turn on of each phase. If the first LED 'D1' is on, it indicates that phase 'A' is on, turning on of second LED 'D2' indicates that phase 'B' is on and 'D3' and 'D4' LED for phase 'Ā' and 'B̄' respectively. Four resistors of 1kΩ are used to limit the current flowing through the LEDs.

The Unipolar Stepper Motor used for the project has a step angle of 1.8° which means it takes 200 steps for the motor to complete one revolution.

$$\text{No of steps required to complete one revolution} = \frac{\text{Total Angle}}{\text{Step Angle}}$$

$$= \frac{360}{1.8}$$

$$= 200$$

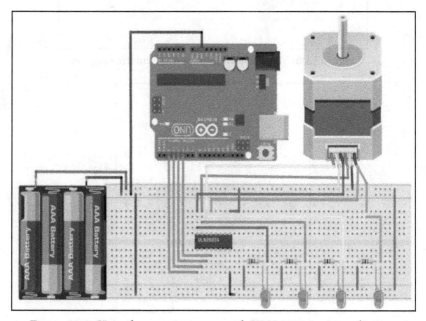

Figure 13.8: Unipolar stepper motor with ULN 2003A wiring diagram

The following program runs the motor with a delay of 0.1 seconds between the turn on of each phase. Since the motor takes a total of 200 steps for a complete revolution, therefore the total time taken by the motor for one revolution is 20 seconds. The speed of the motor is therefore fixed at 3 rpm.

$$\text{Speed of revolution} = \frac{60}{20} = 3 \text{ rpm}$$

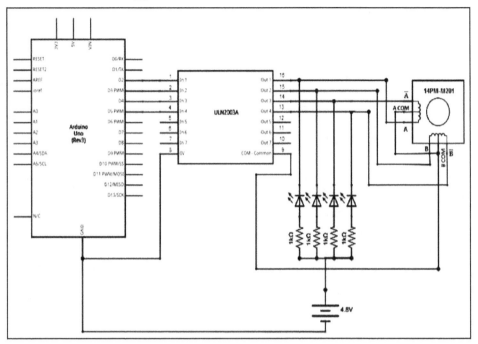

Figure 13.9: Unipolar stepper motor with ULN 2003A schematic diagram

Explanation:

Arduino digital pins 2, 3, 4 and 5 are configured as output pins and are connected to IN1, IN2, IN3 and IN4 pins of ULN 2003A. The excitation of the phases 'A', 'B', '' and '' are therefore controlled by the status setting of Arduino digital pins 2, 3, 4 and 5 respectively. If the digital pin is set HIGH, the corresponding phase is excited and the stepper motor rotates by a step angle.

The commands inside the loop functions gets executed over and over again causing the stepper motor to rotate continuously in a particular direction. In order to reverse the direction of rotation, one needs to edit the program to excite the phases in the sequence 'B̄', 'Ā', 'B' and 'A'. One should also note that the speed of the motor can be varied by altering the delay time between each excitation.

Program:

```
void setup() {
// initialize the digital pin as an output.
pinMode(2, OUTPUT);
pinMode(3, OUTPUT);
pinMode(4, OUTPUT);
pinMode(5, OUTPUT);


}

void loop()
{
digitalWrite(2, HIGH);  //phase A on
delay(100);
digitalWrite(2, LOW);          //phase A off

digitalWrite(3, HIGH);  //phase B on
delay(100);
digitalWrite(3, LOW);          //phase B off

digitalWrite(4, HIGH);  //phase on
delay(100);
digitalWrite(4, LOW);          //phase off

digitalWrite(5, HIGH);  //phase on
delay(100);
digitalWrite(5, LOW);          //phase off
}
//end
```

Project 13.4: Unipolar stepper motor speed control using ULN2003A

In the earlier setup, the program was so written that the motor speed was fixed at 3 rpm. A variable speed control is achieved by varying the delay time for which each phase is kept on. A potentiometer is used to control and vary the on period of each phase. The minimum and maximum value of delay time is fixed between 20 msec and 500 msec in the program. The variable terminal of the potentiometer is connected to analog pin A0 of Arduino board. The speed of the stepper motor correspondingly increases or decreases as the potentiometer is rotated clockwise or counter clockwise.

The increase and decrease of the motor speed can also be observed with blinking of the LEDs connected to each phase. The LEDs indicates which phase is on for a particular instant.

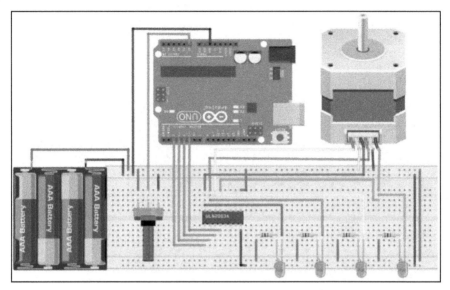

Figure 13.10: Unipolar stepper motor with ULN 2003A and potentiometer wiring diagram

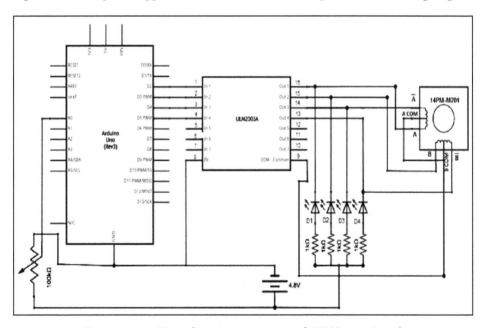

Figure 13.11: Unipolar stepper motor with ULN 2003A and potentiometer schematic diagram

Explanation:

The current position of the potentiometer is continuously read from analog pin A0 and stored in variable 'potValue'. The value so read is mapped in the range '20' to '500' and is updated to variable 'delay_time'. This value decides the current speed of motor rotation.

Program:

```
int potPin = A0; //initialize analog pin A0 as potPin
int potValue = 0; //variable potValue to store data at
analog pin A0
int delay_time=0; //variable to store current delay time

void setup()
{
// initialize the digital pin as an output.
pinMode(2, OUTPUT);
pinMode(3, OUTPUT);
pinMode(4, OUTPUT);
pinMode(5, OUTPUT);
}

void loop()
{
potValue = analogRead(potPin); //read the value from analog
pin A0
delay_time=map(potValue,0,1023,20,500); //map the value
read from A0 and store in variable delay_time

digitalWrite(2, HIGH); //phase A on
delay(delay_time);      //pause for the currently set delay_
time
digitalWrite(2, LOW);  //phase A off

digitalWrite(3, HIGH); //phase B on
delay(delay_time); //pause for the currently set delay_time
digitalWrite(3, LOW);  //phase B off

digitalWrite(4, HIGH); //phase on
```

```
delay(delay_time); //pause for the currently set delay_time
digitalWrite(4, LOW);   //phase off

digitalWrite(5, HIGH); //phase on
delay(delay_time); //pause for the currently set delay_time
digitalWrite(5, LOW);   //phase off
}
//end
```

Bipolar Stepper Motor

Bipolar Stepper Motor is the second type of Hybrid Stepper Motor having one coil winding per stator phase. The model number of the Bipolar Stepper Motor used for the project is 16PU-M202 having a step angle of 3.75°. This particular Bipolar Stepper Motor has two stator phases with four leads and the rotor is made up of Neodymium magnets.

Unlike Unipolar Stepper Motor, each stator phase of Bipolar Stepper Motor needs to be charged positively and negatively in a specific sequence to precisely rotate the motor in clockwise and counter clockwise direction. In other words, the current flows in both directions through each stator coil. Since the Bipolar Stepper Motor uses the complete coil for excitation and motor rotation, the Bipolar Stepper Motor will be able to produce twice as much torque compared to the Unipolar Stepper Motor for same rating.

Components

- Arduino board

- Bipolar Stepper Motor (16PU-M202)

- L293D

- Resistance (1kΩ)

- Potentiometer (10kΩ)

- Battery 9V

- Push Button

- Breadboard

The specifications of 16PU-M202 Bipolar Stepper Motor is listed below.

Table 14.1: Specifications of Bipolar Stepper Motor (16PU-M202)

S.No	Parameter	Value
1.	Phase Current	0.6A
2.	Resistance	5.5Ω
3.	Inductance	6.3mH
4.	Holding torque	74mN-m
5.	Step Angle	3.75 deg
6.	Rated Voltage	24V

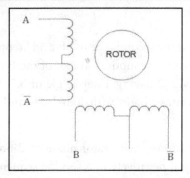

Figure 14.1: Bipolar stepper motor with 4 lead wires

There are three different methods of driving a Bipolar Stepper Motor:

- **Full Step Rotation (1 phase ON):** In this method, only one of phase either phase A or phase B is energized at any given time. The motor rotates at full step angle for each switching sequence. Since only one phase is energized at a time, this type of stepping will give less holding torque compared to the next method Full Step Rotation (2 phase ON).

- **Full Step Rotation (2 phase ON):** Both the phases are energized at every step in a specific sequence to rotate the motor. The motor covers a full step angle for each switching sequence. At every step the rotor align itself in between the two excited stator poles. This method provides more holding torque as both the phases are activated at the same time.

- **Half Step Rotation (1 & 2 phase ON):** In Half Step Rotation method, one phase and two phases are energized alternately to reduce the step angle by half the full step angle. This method can be adopted for precise angle operations. As listed in table 14.4, in step 1 only 1 phase is ON, then in step 2, 2 phases are ON, then again only one phase is ON and the sequence continues. The motor runs with varying torque for every alternate excitation.

Table 14.2: Bipolar stepper motor switching sequence for Full Step rotation (1 phase ON)

Step	A	B
1	+	0
2	0	+
3	—	0
4	0	—

Table 14.3: Bipolar stepper motor switching sequence for Full Step rotation (2 phase ON)

Step	A	B
1	+	—
2	+	+
3	—	+
4	—	—

Table 14.4: Bipolar stepper motor switching sequence for Half Step rotation (1 & 2 phase ON)

Step	A	B
1	+	0
2	+	+
3	0	+
4	—	+
5	—	0
6	—	—
7	0	—
8	+	—

Project 14.1: Bipolar stepper motor control with L293D (1 phase ON)

In order to drive a Bipolar Stepper Motor, we require a bipolar driver or H bridge driver IC to reverse the current direction in the coils of each stator phase. The H bridge IC used for this project is L293D which is convenient to be driven by TTL logic level. L293D must be provided with logic supply voltage of 5 V as well as the voltage at which the motor needs to operate. It is capable of handling a continuous output current of 600 mA. The reader may refer to chapter 7 for further details on L293D. Other H bridge ICs such as SN754410NE and L298 with rated continuous output current of 1A and 2A respectively can also be used._

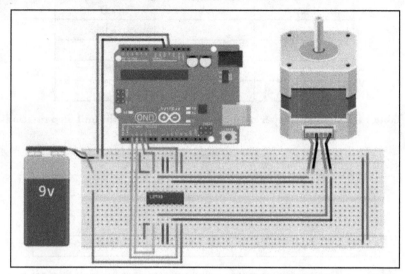

Figure 14.2: Bipolar stepper motor with L293D wiring diagram

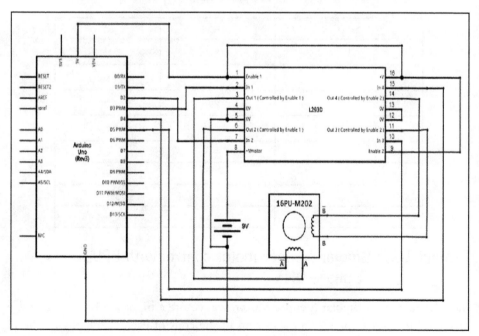

Figure 14.3: Bipolar stepper motor with L293D schematic diagram

Explanation:

The first example is the basic code to make the motor run in one direction for Full Step rotation (1 phase ON) mode. This means only one phase will be ON at a time and L293D motor driver IC is used to control Bipolar Stepper Motor 16PU-M202. Phase 'A', '', 'B' and '' are connected to Output 1, Output 2, Output 3 and Output 4 respectively of L293D. Output 1 and Output 2 is controlled by Enable 1 and Output 3 and Output 4 by Enable 2. Both the Enable pins need to be set HIGH (+5V) in order to activate the output pins. As shown in figure 14.3, Enable 1 and Enable 2 is connected to +5V from Arduino board.

Arduino digital pins '2' and '3' controls the excitation of phase 'A'. When digital pin '2' is set HIGH and digital pin '3' is set LOW, phase 'A' is positive, which means current flows from 'A' to ''. Current reverses its direction i.e. from '' to 'A' for HIGH at digital pin '3' and LOW at digital pin '2'. If both the digital pins '2' and '3' are set at the same logic level i.e. either both HIGH and both LOW, then phase 'A' is off. In other words, there is no flow of current in phase 'A'. Similar control of phase 'B' can be obtained through Arduino digital pins '4' and '5'. The sequence of excitation followed is illustrated in table 14.2.

All the ground pins of L293D IC, Arduino board and 9V power supply is connected together to form a common node.

Program:

```
void setup()
{
// initialize the digital pin as an output.
pinMode(2, OUTPUT);
pinMode(3, OUTPUT);
pinMode(4, OUTPUT);
pinMode(5, OUTPUT);
}

void loop()
{
digitalWrite(2, HIGH);        //phase A positive
digitalWrite(3, LOW);         //phase Ā negative
digitalWrite(4, LOW);         //phase B off
digitalWrite(5, LOW);         //phase B̄ off
delay(100);
digitalWrite(4, HIGH);        //phase B positive
```

```
digitalWrite(5, LOW);          //phase B̄ negative
digitalWrite(2, LOW);          //phase A off
digitalWrite(3, LOW);          //phase Ā off
delay(100);
digitalWrite(2, LOW );         //phase A negative
digitalWrite(3, HIGH);         //phase Ā positive
digitalWrite(4, LOW);          //phase B off
digitalWrite(5, LOW);          //phase off
delay(100);
digitalWrite(4, LOW);          //phase B negative
digitalWrite(5, HIGH);         //phase B̄ positive
digitalWrite(2, LOW);          //phase A off
digitalWrite(3, LOW);          //phase Ā off
delay(100);
}
//end
```

Project 14.2: Bipolar stepper motor control with L293D (2 phase ON)

The next project energizes both the phases at every sequential step to run the motor in a particular direction. This mode of rotation operation is called Full Step rotation (2 phase ON) mode. The motor covers a full step angle at every step of excitation with almost double the holding torque compared to 1 phase ON mode. The full step angle of Bipolar Stepper Motor 16PU-M202 3.75 degrees, therefore it takes 96 steps to complete one revolution.

$$\text{Steps} = \frac{360° \text{ (One revolution)}}{3.75° \text{ (Full step angle)}}$$

$$= 96$$

Explanation:

Arduino digital pins 2 and 3 controls the excitation of Phase A and pins 4 and 5 controls the excitation of Phase B. The sequence of excitation followed is illustrated in table 14.3.

Program:

```
void setup() {
// initialize the digital pin as an output.
pinMode(2, OUTPUT);
```

```
pinMode(3, OUTPUT);
pinMode(4, OUTPUT);
pinMode(5, OUTPUT);
}

void loop()
{
digitalWrite(2, HIGH);          //phase A positive
digitalWrite(3, LOW);           //phase Ā negative
digitalWrite(4, LOW);           //phase B negative
digitalWrite(5, HIGH);          //phase B̄ positive
delay(100);
digitalWrite(2, HIGH);          //phase A positive
digitalWrite(3, LOW);           //phase Ā negative
digitalWrite(4, HIGH);          //phase B positive
digitalWrite(5, LOW);           //phase negative
delay(100);
digitalWrite(2, LOW );          //phase A negative
digitalWrite(3, HIGH);          //phase Ā positive
digitalWrite(4, HIGH);          //phase B positive
digitalWrite(5, LOW);           //phase B̄ negative
delay(100);
digitalWrite(2, LOW );          //phase A negative
digitalWrite(3, HIGH);          //phase Ā positive
digitalWrite(4, LOW);           //phase B negative
digitalWrite(5, HIGH);          //phase B̄ positive
delay(100);
}
//end
```

Project 14.3: Bipolar stepper motor control with L293D (1 & 2 phase ON)

The following program runs the motor under Half Step rotation (1 & 2 phase ON) mode. The motor covers half the full step angle i.e. 1.875 degrees for every sequential step. This means the motor takes a total of 192 steps to complete one revolution.

$$\text{Steps} = \frac{360° \text{ (One revolution)}}{1.875° \text{ (Full step angle)}} = 192$$

The resolution of the motor angular rotation is improved and can be used in applications which require greater degree of angular accuracy.

Explanation:

Arduino digital pins 2 and 3 controls the excitation of Phase A and pins 4 and 5 controls the excitation of Phase B. The sequence of excitation followed is illustrated in table 14.4.

Program:

```
void setup() {
// initialize the digital pin as an output.
pinMode(2, OUTPUT);
pinMode(3, OUTPUT);
pinMode(4, OUTPUT);
pinMode(5, OUTPUT);
}

void loop()
{
digitalWrite(2, HIGH);      //phase A positive
digitalWrite(3, LOW);       //phase Ā negative
digitalWrite(4, LOW);       //phase B off
digitalWrite(5, LOW);       //phase B̄ off
delay(100);
digitalWrite(2, HIGH);      //phase A positive
digitalWrite(3, LOW);       //phase Ā negative
digitalWrite(4, HIGH);      //phase B positive
digitalWrite(5, LOW);       //phase B̄ negative
delay(100);
digitalWrite(2, LOW);       //phase A off
digitalWrite(3, LOW);       //phase Ā off
digitalWrite(4, HIGH);      //phase B positive
digitalWrite(5, LOW);       //phase B̄ negative
delay(100);
digitalWrite(2, LOW);       //phase A negative
```

```
digitalWrite(3, HIGH);        //phase A̅ positive
digitalWrite(4, HIGH);        //phase B positive
digitalWrite(5, LOW);         //phase B̅ negative
delay(100);
digitalWrite(2, LOW);         //phase A negative
digitalWrite(3, HIGH);        //phase A̅ positive
digitalWrite(4, LOW);         //phase B off
digitalWrite(5, LOW);         //phase B̅ off
delay(100);
digitalWrite(2, LOW);         //phase A negative
digitalWrite(3, HIGH);        //phase A̅ positive
digitalWrite(4, LOW);         //phase B negative
digitalWrite(5, HIGH);        //phase B̅ positive
delay(100);
digitalWrite(2, LOW);         //phase A off
digitalWrite(3, LOW);         //phase A̅ off
digitalWrite(4, LOW);         //phase B negative
digitalWrite(5, HIGH);        //phase B̅ positive
delay(100);
digitalWrite(2, HIGH);        //phase A positive
digitalWrite(3, LOW);         //phase A̅ negative
digitalWrite(4, LOW);         //phase B negative
digitalWrite(5, HIGH);        //phase B̅ positive
}
//end
```

Project 14.4: Bipolar Stepper Motor speed and Direction control with L293D

The final example is coded in a more complex way, but allows the motor to spin at different speeds controlled from a potentiometer. The setup below also allows the direction control of the motor using a push button. When the push button is open, digital pin 6 is connected to ground (LOW) terminal and the motor is made to rotate in counter clockwise rotation. On closing the push button, digital pin 6 is set to +5V (HIGH) and the motor rotates in clockwise direction. These two conditions are used in the program to change/decide the direction of rotation of the motor.

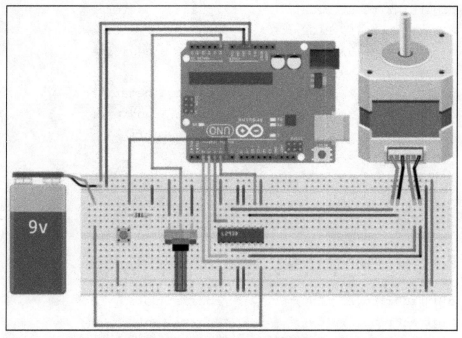

Figure 14.4: Bipolar stepper motor with L293D for direction and speed control wiring diagram

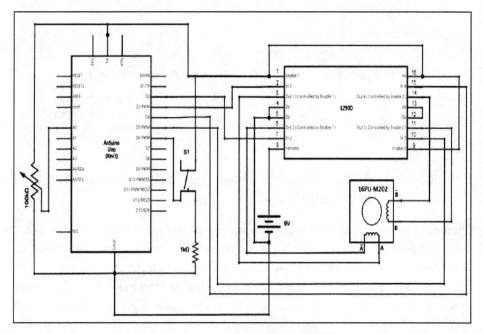

Figure 14.5: Bipolar stepper motor with L293D for direction and speed control schematic diagram

Explanation:

The variable terminal of the potentiometer is connected to analog pin 'A0' of the Arduino board. The analog voltage at 'A0' is read and stored in the variable 'potValue'. This integer value is accordingly mapped between '20' to '500' to adjust the delay time between each sequential step. A high value of delay time between each step decreases the speed of the motor rotation and vice versa. The following program runs the motor under Full Step rotation (2 phase ON) mode.

Program:

```
int potPin = A0; //initialize analog pin A0 as potPin
int potValue = 0; //variable potValue to store data at
analog pin A0
int delay_time=0; //variable to store current delay time

void setup() {
// initialize the digital pin as an output.
pinMode(2, OUTPUT);
pinMode(3, OUTPUT);
pinMode(4, OUTPUT);
pinMode(5, OUTPUT);
pinMode(6, INPUT);
}

void loop()
{
potValue = analogRead(potPin); //read the value from analog
pin A0
delay_time=map(potValue,0,1023,20,500); //map the value
read from A0 and store in variable delay_time

if(digitalRead(6)==HIGH) //clockwise rotation
{
digitalWrite(2, HIGH);    //phase A positive
digitalWrite(3, LOW);     //phase A̅ negative
digitalWrite(4, LOW);     //phase B negative
digitalWrite(5, HIGH);    //phase B̅ positive
delay(delay_time);
digitalWrite(2, HIGH);    //phase A positive
digitalWrite(3, LOW);     //phase A̅ negative
digitalWrite(4, HIGH);    //phase B positive
```

```
digitalWrite(5, LOW);    //phase B̄ negative
delay(delay_time);
digitalWrite(2, LOW );   //phase A negative
digitalWrite(3, HIGH);   //phase Ā positive
digitalWrite(4, HIGH);   //phase B positive
digitalWrite(5, LOW);    //phase B̄ negative
delay(delay_time);
digitalWrite(2, LOW );   //phase A negative
digitalWrite(3, HIGH);   //phase Ā positive
digitalWrite(4, LOW);    //phase B negative
digitalWrite(5, HIGH);   //phase B̄ positive
delay(delay_time);
}


if(digitalRead(6)==LOW)//counter clockwise rotation
{
digitalWrite(2, LOW );   //phase A negative
digitalWrite(3, HIGH);   //phase Ā positive
digitalWrite(4, LOW);    //phase B negative
digitalWrite(5, HIGH);   //phase B̄ positive
delay(delay_time);
digitalWrite(2, LOW );   //phase A negative
digitalWrite(3, HIGH);   //phase Ā positive
digitalWrite(4, HIGH);   //phase B positive
digitalWrite(5, LOW);    //phase B̄ negative
delay(delay_time);
digitalWrite(2, HIGH);   //phase A positive
digitalWrite(3, LOW);    //phase Ā negative
digitalWrite(4, HIGH);   //phase B positive
digitalWrite(5, LOW);    //phase B̄ negative
delay(delay_time);
digitalWrite(2, HIGH);   //phase A positive
digitalWrite(3, LOW);    //phase Ā negative
digitalWrite(4, LOW);    //phase B negative
digitalWrite(5, HIGH);   //phase B̄ positive
delay(delay_time);
}
}
//end
```

Chapter Fifteen

SERIAL COMMUNICATION

In this project, we will learn about serial communication (also known as UART) and understand how it is used for communication between Arduino and a computer. As the name implies, serial communications means sending and receiving data bit by bit over a single line. Arduino Uno board has one serial port at digital pins 0(RX) and 1(TX) to communicate with other external serial devices or with computer through USB cable. The process of sending and receiving data can be observed by the flashing of RX and TX LEDs on the Arduino board.

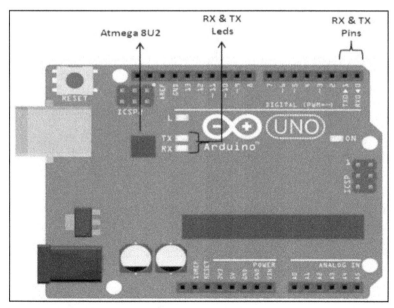

Figure 15.1: Arduino Uno board showing RX and TX pins

In case of serial communication between Arduino and computer, digital pins 0 and 1 should not be used as digitals I/O pins. The Atmega 8U2 chip on Arduino board acts as a bridge between the computer and Arduino processor. It runs on software called firmware that can be updated through a special protocol called DFU (Device Firmware Update).

Components

- Arduino Board

- UBS Cable

Project 15.1: Serial communication between Arduino and Computer

The communication between Arduino and computer is established at a certain baud rate. Baud rate specifies how fast data is sent over a serial line or in other words the speed of serial communication. Some common rates for UART communications are 9600 baud, 19200 baud, 57600 baud and 115200 baud. To start serial communication, the baud rate set for Arduino and computer must be same. If the baud rate for both is set at 9600, then to transmit 1 bit data it would take 1/9600 = 0.104msec.

Explanation:

Let us first try to write a simple program to send a character from computer to Arduino and receive it back by the computer. Firstly we need to connect the Arduino board to any USB port of your computer and upload the following sketch to the Arduino board.

The program starts with opening the serial communication between Arduino processor (microcontroller) and computer using serial function 'Serial.begin(9600)' at baud rate of 9600 bps. Another important function is 'Serial.available( )' which returns the number of bytes that are currently present in the Arduino serial buffer.

The 'while' loop in the program continues to wait until any serial data is received from the computer. If any byte of data is sent from the computer, the data will be available in the serial buffer of the Arduino and the 'while' loop breaks as 'Serial.available( )' function will return a value greater than '0'. If serial data is available, the next step is to read the data using 'Serial.read( )' function and store it in a character variable called 'value'.

After the data sent from the computer is received by the Arduino processor, we want the received data to be sent back to the computer. The function which helps us to do this is 'Serial.println( )'. This function prints data to the serial port to which Arduino is connected.

Upload the following sketch to your Arduino and click on the right most icon on the toolbar in the Arduino IDE (Integrated development environment).

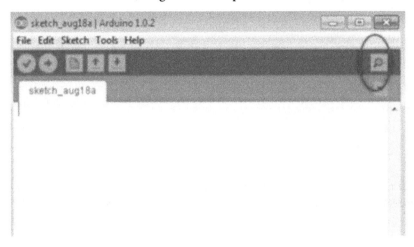

This will open a window which is called Serial Monitor.

Serial monitor is a part of Arduino IDE and allows the user to send data from computer to the Arduino board as well as receive and show data received from the Arduino board.

After the uploading of the program, write character '0' in the edit box of the Serial Monitor and click on the send button. This means we are sending character '0' from computer to the Arduino board.

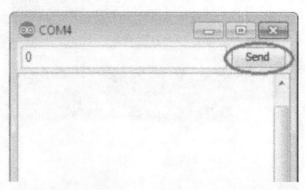

According the program uploaded in the Arduino, it prints (sends) data back to the computer. So we receive a data on the Serial Monitor as shown below.

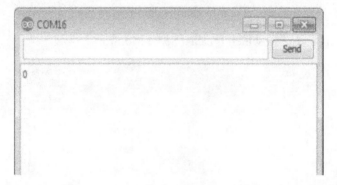

Repeat the same for characters '1', '2', '3', '4' and '5' and the Serial Monitor appears as shown.

As seen above, we are getting back the same character in response to the character sent to the Arduino board.

Program:

```
char value; //initialize variable 'value'

void setup()
{
  Serial.begin(9600); //start serial communication with
computer at 9600 baud rate
}

void loop()
{
  while(Serial.available()==0); //wait for serial data
  value=Serial.read(); //read the serial data(ASCII value)
  Serial.println(value); //print the value back to serial
monitor(computer)
}
//end
```

Project 15.2: LED control through Serial Communication

Let us further extend the above program to control the inbuilt LED on the Arduino board connected to digital pin '13' through Serial Monitor. The following program turns ON the LED when character '1' is received by the Arduino processor and sends back a string 'LED is ON' as acknowledgement to the Serial Monitor. On receiving character '0', the Arduino turns OFF the inbuilt LED and sends back an acknowledgement 'LED is OFF'.

Explanation:

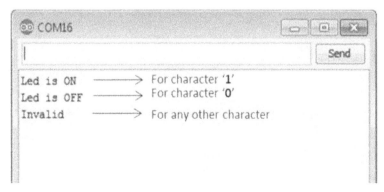

On sending character '0' to Arduino, the LED is turned off and simultaneously string 'LED in OFF' is displayed on the Serial Monitor. Arduino will send string 'Invalid' to the Serial Monitor for any other character except '1' and '0' and the state of the LED will remain unchanged.

Not only single characters, we can also send strings or a group of strings from the Serial Monitor to Arduino processor at one go by pressing the send button. The same can be displayed on a LCD/ Dot Matrix display or can even be used as command to perform a task.

Program:

```
char value;        //initialize variable 'value'
int LED =13;       //initialize variable 'LED'


void setup()
{
 Serial.begin(9600);    //start serial communication with
computer at 9600 baud rate
 pinMode(LED,OUTPUT);   //initialize digital pin 13 as
output
}


void loop()
{
 while(Serial.available()==0); //wait for serial data
 value=Serial.read(); //read the serial data(ASCII value)

 if(value=='0') //if data received is decimal '0'
 {
 digitalWrite(LED,LOW); //turn on LED
 Serial.println("LED is OFF"); //print 'LED is OFF' on the
serial monitor(computer)
 }


 else if(value=='1') //if data received is decimal '1'
 {
 digitalWrite(LED,HIGH); //turn off LED
 Serial.println("LED is ON"); //print 'LED is ON' on the
serial monitor(computer)
 }
```

```
else//if data received is neither decimal '0' or '1'
{
Serial.println("Invalid"); //print 'Invalid' on the serial
monitor(computer)
}
}

//end
```

hapter **Sixteen**

Wireless Communication Using XBee

This project will demonstrate simple data transmission by sending data from one Arduino board to other wirelessly using XBee modules. XBee's are product names for radio communications modules made by Digi. The XBee modules are popular because they are readily available from distributors and relatively easy to add to embedded designs. They are also most convenient and easy to use with Arduino Uno board to transmit and receive data wirelessly over greater range at high speed.

The XBee RF Modules implements ZigBee or 802.15.4 protocol and are available in many versions (Series 1, Series 2 and Pro) and power ratings. But the XBee's of different versions are not compatible with each other for data transmission. For the project, two XBee Series 1 transceivers are used for wireless communication. The Series 1 module operates at 2.4 GHz frequency.

Figure 16.1: XBee Series 1

Components

- Arduino board

- XBee Series 1 module

- XBee Explorer

- Push Button

- Potentiometer (10kΩ)

- Servo Motor

- Breadboard

These are the easiest to work with and they don't need to be configured. Because they are easy to work with, these are recommended for those who are just starting with wireless RF communication.

The important technical specifications of modules from XBee family are listed.

Module	Performance			
	Indoor Range	Outdoor Range	Transmit Power	RF Data Rate
XBee Series 1	100 ft (30 m)	300 ft (100 m)	1 mW	250 kbps
XBee Series 2	133 ft (40 m)	400 ft. (120 m)	2mW	250 kbps
XBee Pro	1200 ft (370 m)	Up to 6 mi (9.6 km)	100 mW	250 kbps

All the XBee modules are provided with 20 pins which comprises of 6 10-bit ADC input pins, 8 digital I/O pins and power pins (3.3V and GND). But the modules have smaller pin spacing than most breadboards. Because of this, it is more convenient to interface the modules with Arduino board using XBee Explorer.

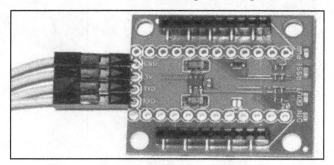

Figure 16.2: XBee Explorer

The XBee module fits perfectly on the XBee explorer and then can be directly connected to a breadboard or Arduino board. Take care of the orientation while placing the module on the explorer board else the module can be damaged permanently. Place the module on the explorer board as shown below.

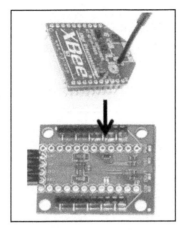

Figure 16.3: Placing XBee on Explorer board

Project 16.1: Wireless control of inbuilt LED using XBee

Firstly the project will demonstrate simple data transmission between two XBee's. Two XBee modules are connected to the Arduino boards after placing them on XBee Explorer boards. The XBee modules will communicate via serial line of the Arduino Uno board. Here the RX and TX pin of XBee Explorer is connected to the TX and RX pin of Arduino Uno board respectively.

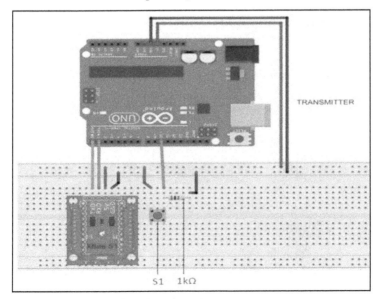

Figure 16.4: Transmitter setup using XBee Series 1 Explorer and Arduino wiring diagram

An XBee Series 1 module can work both as a transmitter and receiver at the same time. However, we will try to send a string of data from one module (transmitter) to another module (receiver) and control the LED at pin 13 of the Arduino board at the receiver end. When the push button in the transmitter setup is pressed, the inbuilt LED at pin 13 in the receiver setup should turn ON. On releasing the push button, the LED should turn OFF. This is an example of wireless control.

There are two different programs and wiring diagrams for transmitter and receiver setup.

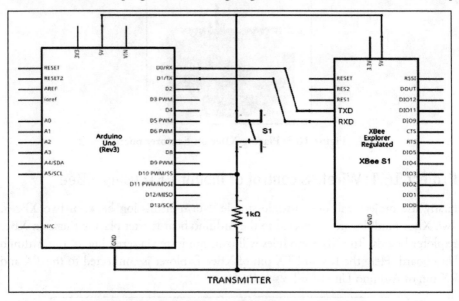

Figure 16.5: Transmitter setup using XBee Series 1 Explorer and Arduino schematic diagram

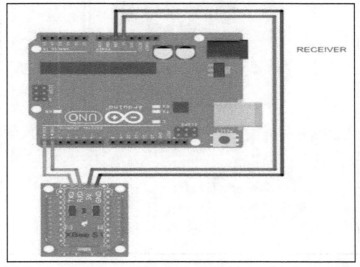

Figure 16.6: Receiver setup using XBee Series 1 Explorer and Arduino wiring diagram

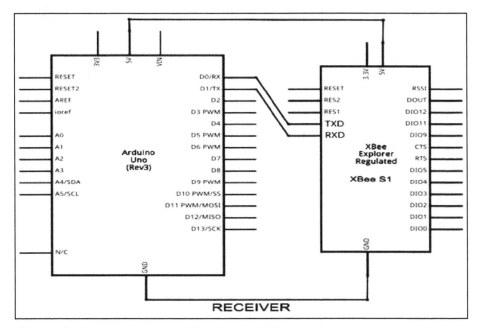

Figure 16.7: Receiver setup using XBee Series 1 Explorer and Arduino schematic diagram

Explanation:

Upload the transmitter and receiver programs on the two separate Arduino boards before doing the XBee connections. The transmitter circuit uses a pushbutton which when pressed sets 5V at digital pin 10 and 0V on release. This is used as a condition to send characters 'H' and 'L' to the receiver XBee through the serial port. On pressing the button, the microcontroller on the Arduino board writes character 'H' on the serial port (digital pins 0 and 1). The transmitter XBee thereby transmits the character to the receiver end XBee. Character 'L' is transmitted when the button is released.

The receiver XBee continuously receives serial data at 9600 baud rate. The Arduino microcontroller in the receiver end monitors the availability of data on the serial port. If the data is available, it is stored in character variable 'c'. The program turns the LED at digital pin 13 if the character variable is 'H' and turn off the LED if the variable is updated to character 'L'.

Instead of keeping both the Arduino boards connected through USB port for power supply, the receiver side Arduino can be powered with a 9V battery for performing XBee range test.

Program:

```
//transmitter
const int buttonPin = 10; // the number of the pushbutton pin
```

```
int buttonState = 0; // variable for reading the pushbutton
status

void setup()
{
 Serial.begin(9600); // Open serial communication port
pinMode(buttonPin, INPUT); // initialize the pushbutton pin
as an input
 }

void loop()
{
 buttonState = digitalRead(buttonPin); // read the state of
the pushbutton value
 if (buttonState == HIGH) // if it is, the buttonState is HIGH
 {
 Serial.println('H'); //write character 'H' to serial line
(XBee)
 }
 else {
 Serial.println('L');  //write character 'L' to serial line
(XBee)
 }
 delay(100);
}
//end
```

Next is the program which needs to be uploaded on the receiver side Arduino board.

```
//receiver
int LED = 13; // the number of the LED pin

void setup()
{
Serial.begin(9600); // Open serial communication port
 pinMode(LED, OUTPUT); // initialize the LED pin as an
output
}

void loop()
```

```
{
 while(Serial.available()==0); //wait till data is available
in the serial port
 char c=Serial.read(); //read the serial data

 if(c=='H') //if the serial data is 'H'
 {
 digitalWrite(LED, HIGH); // turn the LED on
 }
 if(c=='L') //if the serial data is 'H'
 {
 digitalWrite(LED, LOW); // turn the LED off
 }
 }
//end
```

Project 16.2: Wireless control of Servomotor using XBee

Next we will go through the process of controlling a servo motor wirelessly. A potentiometer (P1) is hooked up to one Arduino (Transmitter) and servo motor to another Arduino (Receiver). The two Arduino's communicate with each other wirelessly using XBee modules. The rotation of the servo motor on the receiver side follows the movement of the potentiometer on the transmitter side.

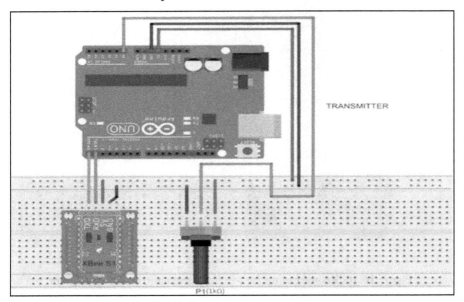

Figure 16.8: Transmitter setup for wireless servo control wiring diagram

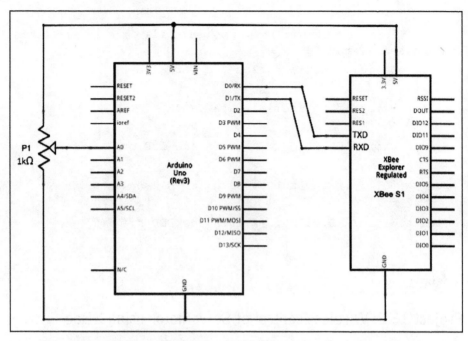

Figure 16.9: Transmitter setup for wireless servo control schematic diagram

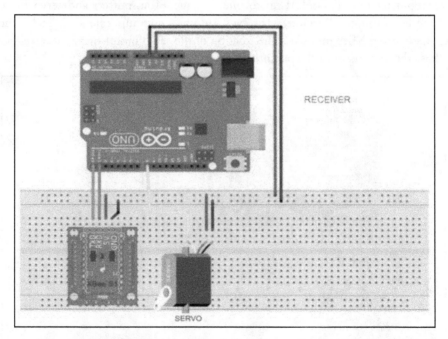

Figure 16.10: Receiver setup for wireless servo control wiring diagram

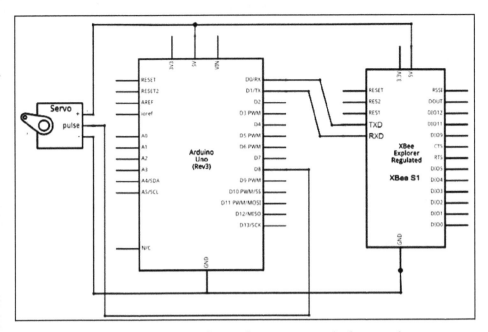

Figure 16.11: Receiver setup for wireless servo control schematic diagram

Explanation:

The program controls the movement of a servo motor attached to digital pin 8 in the receiver end. The movement is decided by the serial data received between 0 and 9. Hence the motor can hold at 10 different positions.

In the transmitter end, a potentiometer is read by the Arduino from analog pin 'A0' and the value so read is scaled between 0 and 9. This is done to maintain the simplicity of the program. Based on the position of the potentiometer, the transmitter sends the corresponding value to the receiver.

We can use the idea to build a wirelessly controlled robotic arm or achieve control of any other device in the receiver end. Remember to use a separate 5V battery to operate the servo motor for running under load conditions.

Program:

```
//transmitter
int sensorPin = A0; // select the input pin for the
potentiometer
int potValue; // variable to store the value coming from
the potentiometer

void setup()
```

```
{
  Serial.begin(9600); //start serial communication
}


void loop()
{
  potValue = analogRead(sensorPin); // read the value from
the potentiometer
  potValue = map(potValue, 0, 1023, 0, 9); //map the value
between 0 to 9
  Serial.println(potValue); //write the value to the serial
port
  delay(50);
  }
//end
```

Next is the program which needs to be uploaded on the receiver side Arduino board.

```
#include <Servo.h>
Servo myServo; // create servo object to control a servo
int data; // variable to read the value from serial port


void setup()
{
  Serial.begin(9600);
  myServo.attach(8); // attach the servo on pin 8
}


void loop()
{
  while(Serial.available()==0); //wait till data is available
in the serial port
  data = Serial.read()-'0'; //read the serial data
  data=map(data, 0, 9, 0, 180); // scale it to use it with
the servo (value between 0 and 180)


  myServo.write(data); // sets the servo position according
to the scaled value


}
//end
```

Infrared Remote Control

In this chapter we'll learn how to send and receive data using Infrared (IR) transmitter and receiver module. The TV remote control that we use daily is an example of the application of Infrared remote control. The IR signal is sent from the remote control whenever any button is pressed and thereby received by an IR sensor in the TV set. Although one should always remember that the remote control should be paced in the line of sight with the IR sensor.

IR remote control uses an ordinary TV remote and TSOP (Thin Small Outline Package) as IR sensor. We'll use a Panasonic TV remote like the one shown in figure 17.1. When a key is pressed, the IR LED in the remote control turns ON and OFF in a particular pattern and transmits data at a carrier frequency of 30-40 kHz. The pattern associated with each key on the remote is different.

Figure 17.1: Panasonic TV remote control

Components

- Arduino board

- TSOP 1738

- Remote Control

- Resistance (1kΩ)

- LED

- Breadboard

The TSOP module is used at the receiving end of an IR remote control system. Continuous data transmission is possible using TSOP's with added advantages of low power consumption and high immunity against ambient light. TSOP's are available for different carrier frequencies. TSOP 1738 with 38 kHz carrier frequency is used.

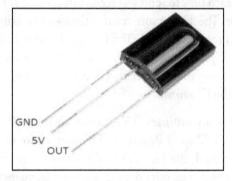

GND

5V

OUT

Figure 17.2: TSOP 1738.

TSOP modules receives modulated signal and gives out demodulated signal. They are designed to work as an IR filter such that its output signal can easily be decoded using microcontrollers. This means TSOP outputs logic-level signals. TSOP 1738 module works in the active-low configuration and its output would normally remain high. The demodulated output would go low when it detects any signal from the remote control.

Panasonic remote control sends message using RECS-80 protocol. Every time you press a button on a Panasonic remote control, it sends out a 32 bit data. The first 8 bits indicates thee address code followed by the inverse of the address code. The next 8 bits are the command code which will vary depending upon the keys being pressed. The command code is followed by the inverse of it. The inverse transmitted bits are very useful for the error detection. The address codes will be same for all the buttons but may vary for different devices.

Figure 17.3 shows the demodulated output of TSOP. The output consists of random combination of high signals (called marks) and the low signal (spaces). The signal is normally high but once data is received, the output goes low for 4T period. This indicates the start of data transmission. For logic '1', the duration of the low signal (space) is 3T and T for logic '0'. Each space is separated by a mark of period T, where T=0.42 msec.

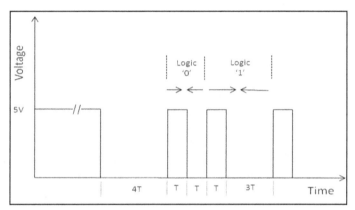

Figure 17.3: TSOP demodulated output sample

Project 17.1: Receiving Command Codes for Infrared remote Control

Before proceeding with the project, one needs to know the command codes for different buttons on the remote control. As an example we will be using only three buttons on the remote control and the first job is to get the command codes. Here we will be testing with buttons '1', '2' and '3' on the remote control.

The figures below illustrates the wiring and schematic diagram required for the project.

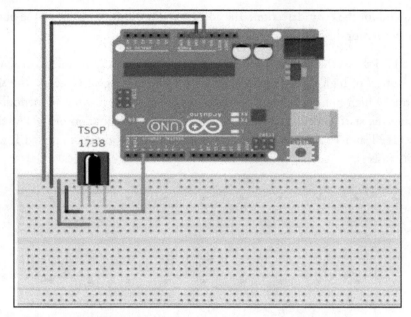

Figure 17.4: TSOP with Arduino for receiving data wiring diagram

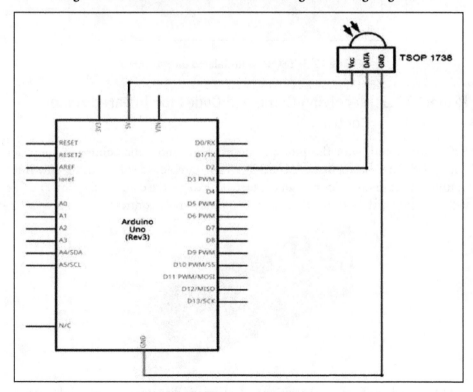

Figure 17.5: TSOP with Arduino for receiving data schematic diagram

Explanation:

The setup allows stable and secure transmission of data using infrared technology. After connecting your TSOP (IR receiver) to the Arduino pin 2, upload the sketch and observe the output in the serial monitor. This sketch prints the code on the serial monitor every time a button on the remote control is pressed. On pressing the buttons '1', '2' and '3' on the remote control, the corresponding command code gets displayed on the serial monitor.

The output on the serial monitor in hexadecimal is shown below.

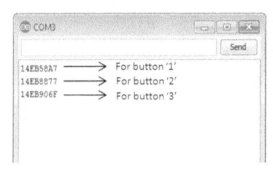

For all the buttons the address code and its inverse is same i.e. '14EB'. But the command codes vary with every button pressed. For button 1 on the remote control the command code and its inverse received is '58A7' and for button 2 it is '8877' and so on. So we can use individual buttons for doing different task.

The command codes are easily decoded using 'IRremote' library. The IRrecv class performs the decoding process and is initialized with enableIRIn() function. The serial communication with the PC is also started so that we are able to use the serial monitor. Inside the loop function, the 'decode()' function is called to check the availability of data at digital pin 2. It returns a nonzero value if the data is available. The decoded data can be read from decode_results structure. The 'resume()' function is called after the completion of each decoding process to resume receiving next set of codes.

Program:

```
#include <IRremote.h> //include infrared library
int RECV_PIN = 2; //declare digital pin 2 as the receiving pin
IRrecv irrecv(RECV_PIN); //create instance of irrecv
decode_results results;

void setup()
{
  Serial.begin(9600); //start serial communication
```

```
irrecv.enableIRIn(); // start the infrared receiver
}
void loop()
{

if (irrecv.decode(&results)) //on receiving IR signal
{
Serial.println(results.value, HEX); //display the decoded
data on the serial monitor
irrecv.resume(); //receive the next value
}

delay(100);

}

//end
```

Project 17.2: LED control using Infrared Technology

This project will demonstrate how to control digital output pins using IR remote control. The following sketch will allow us to control three LEDs connected at digital pins 8, 9 and 10 with the remote control buttons 1, 2, and 3 respectively.

The wiring diagram is similar to the earlier project for testing IR data transmission.

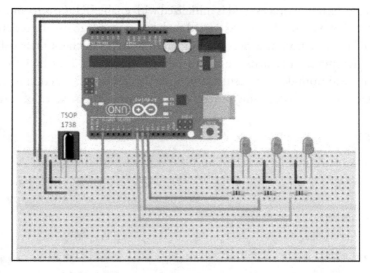

Figure 17.6: Three LED control using IR remote control wiring diagram

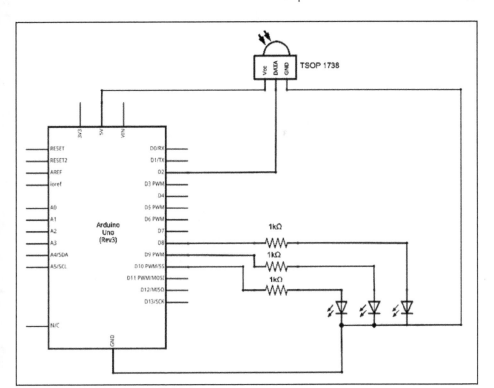

Figure 17.7: Three LED control using IR remote control schematic diagram

Explanation:

On further expanding the above sketch, we will be able to control three LEDs connected to Arduino digital pins 8, 9 and 10 using buttons 1, 2 and 3 on the remote control. We have already captured the hexadecimal command code for the three buttons and are used in a switch statement to identify the button pressed.

On pressing button 1 on the remote control, LED connected to digital pin 8 turns ON for a second. Similarly the LEDs connected to digital pins 9 and 10 turns ON by pressing buttons 2 and 3 respectively. The sketch can be changed to control a four wheeler ROBOT by making the necessary changes.

An additional 'check()' function is added to the earlier sketch to identify which button is pressed on the remote control. The hexadecimal value '14EB58A7' resembles button 1, '14EB8877' resembles button 2 and '14EB906F' button 3 respectively. On receiving the code, the corresponding LED is turned ON for a second.

Program:

```
#include <IRremote.h> //include infrared library

int RECV_PIN = 2; //declare digital pin 2 as the receiving pin

IRrecv irrecv(RECV_PIN); //create instance of irrecv

decode_results results;

void setup()
{
 Serial.begin(9600);    //start serial communication
 irrecv.enableIRIn();   // start the infrared receiver

 pinMode(8, OUTPUT);
 pinMode(9, OUTPUT);
 pinMode(10, OUTPUT);

}

void loop()
{

 if (irrecv.decode(&results)) //on receiving IR signal
 {
 Serial.println(results.value, HEX);
//display the decoded data on the serial monitor
 check(); //call the function to identify the button pressed
 irrecv.resume(); // Receive the next value
 }


}
void check()
{
 switch(results.value)
 {
 case 0x14EB58A7:        //if button 1 is pressed
```

```
digitalWrite(8, HIGH);
delay(1000);
digitalWrite(8, LOW);
break;

case 0x14EB8877:       //if button 2 is pressed

digitalWrite(9, HIGH);
delay(1000);
digitalWrite(9, LOW);
break;

case 0x14EB906F:       //if button 3 is pressed

digitalWrite(10, HIGH);
delay(1000);
digitalWrite(10, LOW);
break;

 }
}

//end
```

SD Card Data Logger

The project will cover reading and writing files with the SD card using Arduino Uno. SD memory card comes in large storage capacities ranging up to 32 GB and therefore results in its wide usage for storing data values read by the microcontroller. The size of the EEPROM memory of Arduino Uno is only 1 KB, which is comparatively very small when it comes to storing large data. SD card along with SD card shield is required for interfacing and to start the communication between the SD card and Arduino. Serial Peripheral Interface (SPI) is used to make the SD card shield and Arduino talk with each other.

Components

- Arduino board
- SD Card (4GB)
- SD Card Shield
- DHT11 Sensor
- Breadboard

Project 18.1: Writing text data on SD Card

Micro SD shield is used for the project in which the SD card is inserted and which helps to communicate with the Arduino board to read and write files via SPI interface. SPI is a synchronous serial data protocol used by Arduino for communicating with one or more peripheral devices and can take place on the digital pins 11, 12, and 13 on the Arduino Uno board. It can also be used for communication between two microcontrollers. There must be a master device (Arduino microcontroller) and at least one slave device (peripheral device like SD card shield) in an SPI connection. There are usually four lines linking master and slave devices:

1. **MISO (Master In Slave Out):** Link for sending data from Slave to Master device.

2. **MOSI (Master Out Slave In):** Link for sending data from Master to Slave device.

3. **SCK (Serial Clock):** The clock pulses which synchronize data transmission between Master and Slave device.

4. **CS (Chip Select):** The line used by the Master device to enable or disable a particular Slave device. When the Chip Select (CS) line is LOW, the peripheral device communicates with the Master device. In order to deselect the peripheral device and stop the serial communication the Chip Select line is set HIGH. With the help of CS line the Master device can communicate with more than one SPI devices.

The SD card shield control interface with the Arduino board is illustrated in the following table.

Table 18.1: Interface with Arduino and SD shield

S.No	SD card shield	Arduino board
1.	MISO	Digital pin 12
2.	MOSI	Digital pin 11
3.	SCK	Digital pin 13
4.	CS	Digital pin 10
5.	Vcc	+5V
6.	GND	GND

Arduino IDE comes with SD library, which makes the control of the SD card shield very simple. In other words, the SD library allows reading from and writing to SD cards using its inbuilt functions. The important functions used in the project and their explanations are listed below.

1. `SD.begin()`

The function initializes the SD library and the SD card and begins the use of the SPI bus (digital pins 11, 12, 13 and an additional chip select pin). It returns true on success and false on failure.

2. `SD.exists(filename)`

The function tests whether a file exists on the SD card or not. It returns true if the file exists and false if not.

3. `SD.open(filename, mode)`

The function opens a file on the SD card. If the file is opened for writing, it will be created if it doesn't exist. There are two modes in which the file can be opened i.e. FILE_READ or FILE_WRITE. The default mode in which the file is opened is FILE_READ.

4. `SD.remove(filename)`

Remove a file from the SD card.

5. `file.read()`

Read a byte from the file.

6. `file.write(data)`

Write data to the file.

7. `file.close()`

Close the file, and ensure that any data written to it is physically saved to the SD card.

8. `file.available()`

Check if there are any bytes available for reading from the file.

(file is an instance of the File class)

Now that we have covered the basics, it's time to connect the micro SD shield with the Arduino board.

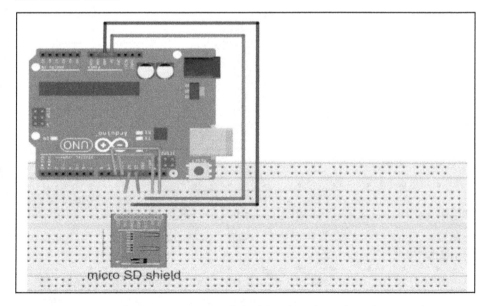

Figure 18.1: Interfacing micro SD card shield with Arduino board wiring diagram

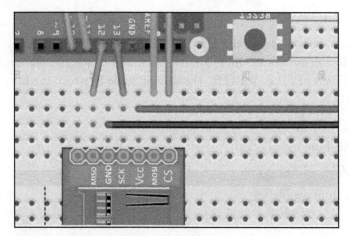

Figure 18.2: Interfacing micro SD card shield with Arduino board wiring diagram (zoomed-in view)

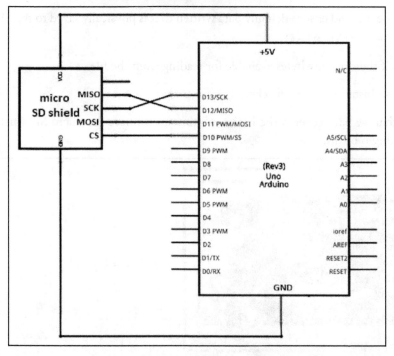

Figure 18.3: Interfacing micro SD card shield with Arduino board schematic diagram

Explanation:

We will start with the process of reading from, and writing to an SD card. We can read or write on text files, word documents and excel worksheets. First let us see how to work on text files.

The following program writes a short message on a text file on the SD card after every 3 seconds. The program begins by including the SD card library which allows us to use all the SD card functions from the library. The MISO, MOSI and SCK pins are already configured in Arduino Uno board. But the chip select pin varies with the SD card shield. The chip select pin is initialized as '10', which means digital pin 10 is connected to the CS pin of the SD card shield. We also need to create a data file object 'myFile' of class file.

Inside the setup function, serial communication between the computer and Arduino is established using 'Serial.begin()' function at 9600 baud rate. This helps us debugging the program and view relevant information on the serial monitor. Before we start writing on a text file, we need to start the initialization process of the SD card using SD function 'SD.begin(CS)'. If the initialization process fails, the 'return' statement terminates the whole program. On successful initialization of the SD card, Arduino prints 'Initialization Completed' on the serial monitor to let the user know about the completion of the process.

Next inside the loop function we need to create and open a text file 'example.txt' using 'SD.open' function in write mode. If the text file doesn't exist in the SD card, the function will create the stated text file. If the data file is created, string 'Test message' is written on the text file 'example.txt' on the SD card. Simultaneously the same string is also printed on the serial monitor, which is also useful for the programmer to debug the program. After doing the writing job, the program saves and closes the text file. The process is repeated and the string is written onto the SD card every three seconds. On the event of the failure of the above process, string 'Error in opening the file' is showed up on the serial monitor.

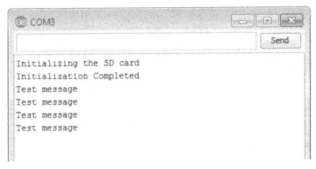

Program:

```
#include <SD.h> // include the SD library
int CS = 10; //initialize chip select pin to 10
File myFile; //create a data file object named 'myFile'

void setup()
```

```
{
 Serial.begin(9600); //start serial communication
 Serial.println("Initializing the SD card");
 if(!SD.begin(CS)) //start SD card via SPI communication
 {
 Serial.println("Initialization Failed !!!");
 return; //exit from the setup function
 }
 Serial.println("Initialization Completed");
 }

void loop()
{
 myFile = SD.open("example.txt", FILE_WRITE); //create and
open a text file

 if(myFile)
 {
 myFile.println("Test message"); //write 'Test message' on
SD card
 Serial.println("Test message"); // write 'Test message' on
Serial monitor
 myFile.close(); //close and save the text file
 }
 else
 {
 Serial.println("Error in opening the file");
//prints on Serial monitor
 }
delay(3000); //delay of 3 sec
}
//end
```

Project 18.2: Reading text data from SD Card

After writing on the SD card, we also need to learn how to read text data from the SD card.

Explanation:

The following program allows us to read the data from the SD card. As an example, in the program a text file 'DATA.txt' is created in the SD card prior to uploading the sketch to Arduino board.

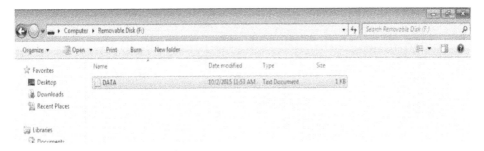

When the text file is opened, the following window shows up

The text file 'DATA.txt' is having two string datas 'ARDUINO' and '1234' which is read by the Arduino microcontroller and simultaneously displays it on the serial monitor. One byte of data is read at a time.

The Arduino program for reading the data from the SD card is similar to the task of writing on the SD card. The change is only inside the loop function. Inside the loop function, the SD card is opened in read mode by default. The while loop reads each byte at a time from the "DATA.txt' file and also prints it on the serial monitor.

After uploading the Arduino program, open the serial monitor to observe the result.

Program:

```
#include <SD.h> // include the SD library
int CS = 10; //initialize chip select pin to 10
File myFile; //create a data file object named 'myFile'

void setup()
{
 Serial.begin(9600); //start serial communication
 Serial.println("Initializing the SD card");
 if(!SD.begin(CS)) //start SD card via SPI communication
{
 Serial.println("Initialization Failed !!!");
 return; //exit from the setup function
}

Serial.println("Initialization Completed");
}
void loop()
{
 myFile = SD.open("DATA.txt"); // open a text file 'DATA.txt'

 if(myFile) //if the text file 'DATA.txt' exists
 {
 while(myFile.available()) //continue till the data is available
 {
 char c = myFile.read(); //read and store the data from text
file in character variable 'c'
 Serial.println(c); //print the read data on the serial monitor
 }
 myFile.close(); //close and save the text file
 }
 else
 {
 Serial.println("Error in opening the file"); //prints on
Serial monitor
 }
 delay(3000); //wait for 3 econds
}
 //end
```

Project 18.3: Writing text data to CSV file on SD card

Instead of writing data's on a text file, sometimes it is more advantageous to write on Excel sheets. The SD card library uses CSV file format to store tabular data similar to Microsoft Excel. CSV stands for "Comma Separated Values". The fields of data in each row are delimited or separated with a comma and individual rows are separated by a newline.

Explanation:

So, in the next section we shall learn how to write data on a CSV file. Here the program is similar to the earlier program for writing on a text file. The 'SD.open' function opens a CSV file 'DATA.csv'. On the absence of the particular file, the function creates 'DATA.csv' file.

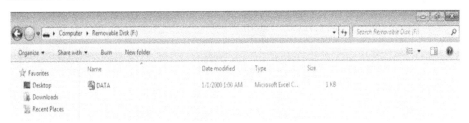

Once the file is opened, the Arduino microcontroller writes string 'DATA 1' in the first column and 'DATA 2' in the next column. By printing a comma character on the CSV file, the column on which the second string is written gets shifted by one.

The following program writes on a CSV file in the following manner.

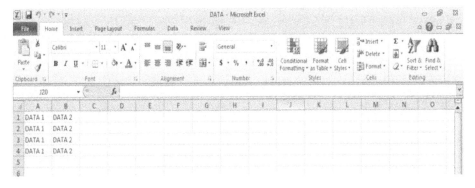

Program:

```
#include <SD.h> // include the SD library
int CS = 10; //initialize chip select pin to 10
File myFile; //create a data file object named 'myFile'
```

```
void setup()
{
 Serial.begin(9600); //start serial communication
 Serial.println("Initializing the SD card");
 if(!SD.begin(CS)) //start SD card via SPI communication
 {
 Serial.println("Initialization Failed !!!");
 return; //exit from the setup function
 }
Serial.println("Initialization Completed");
 }


void loop()
{
 myFile = SD.open("DATA.csv", FILE_WRITE); // open a csv
file 'DATA.csv'

 if(myFile)
 {
 myFile.print("DATA 1"); //write 'DATA 1' on SD card
 myFile.print(","); //shift to next column
 myFile.println("DATA 2"); //write 'DATA 2' on SD card
 Serial.println("Writing on SD card Complete"); //prints on
Serial monitor
 myFile.close(); //close and save the text file
 }
 else
 {
 Serial.println("Error in opening the file"); //prints on
Serial monitor
 }
 delay(3000); //wait for 3 seconds
}
//end
```

Project 18.4: Interfacing DHT 11 with Arduino

Our next step is to build a data logger for reading temperature and humidity and storing it to the SD card for any given interval. For measuring temperature and humidity, DHT11 sensor is used. The DHT11 has three lines: GND, +5V and a single data line.

The sensing element used in DHT 11 sensor is polymer resistor. The measuring range for the sensor is 20 – 90% relative humidity and 0 – 50 °C temperature. Other similar sensors which can be used in replacement of DHT 11 are DHT 22 and RHT 03.

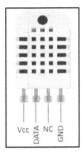

Figure 18.4: DHT11 Temperature and Humidity sensor

Following table illustrates the pin description of DHT11.

Table 18.2: Pin Description of DHT11

Vcc	Supply voltage (+5V)
DATA	Data Line
NC	Not connected
GND	Ground (0V)

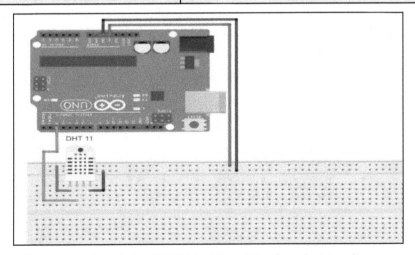

Figure 18.5: Interfacing DHT 11 with Arduino board wiring diagram

The following figures show the wiring and schematic diagram for interfacing SD card and DHT 11 sensor with Arduino Uno board.

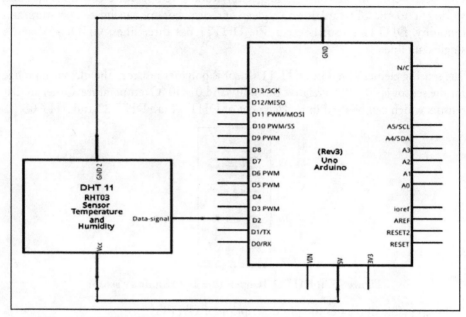

Figure 18.6: Interfacing DHT 11 with Arduino board schematic diagram

Explanation:

To read the DHT 11 sensor for humidity and temperature values, Arduino library 'dht11.h' is used. In the loop function, the current values of humidity and temperature are continuously read through digital pin 2 to which the data line of DHT 11 sensor is connected. The program gets the values of humidity and temperature using commands 'DHT11.humidity' and 'DHT11.temperature'. The readings are also written on the serial monitor.

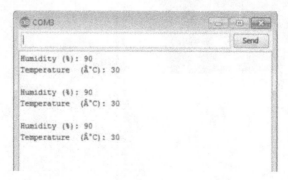

Program:

```
#include <dht11.h> //Include DHT11 library

dht11 DHT11; //create DHT11 object
int Humidity, Temperature; //declare variables to store
values

void setup()
{
 Serial.begin(9600); //begin serial communication
}

void loop()
{

 DHT11.read(2); //read data from digital pin 2

 Humidity=DHT11.humidity; //get the value of humidity from
sensor
    Temperature=DHT11.temperature;   //get   the   value   of
temperature from sensor

 Serial.print("Humidity (%): ");
 Serial.println(Humidity); //print the value of humidity on
serial monitor

 Serial.print("Temperature (°C): ");
    Serial.println(Temperature);   //print   the   value   of
temperature on serial monitor

 Serial.println("");
 delay(2000); //wait for 2 seconds
}
//end
```

Project 18.5: Writing Temperature and Humidity values on SD card

Now that we have the sensor working, let us create a sketch for reading temperature and humidity data at regular intervals and storing it to the SD card. In other words, a data logger to store temperature and humidity data in CSV file.

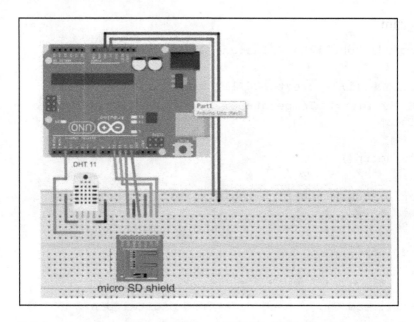

Figure 18.7: Interfacing micro SD card shield and DHT 11 with Arduino board wiring diagram

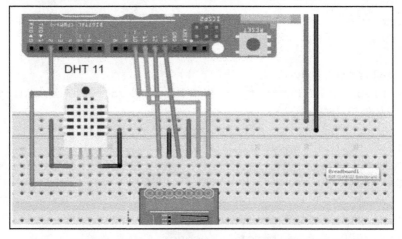

Figure 18.8: Interfacing micro SD card shield and DHT 11 with Arduino board wiring diagram (zoomed-in view)

Explanation:

The following program writes the values of humidity and temperature on the micro SD card shield which can be used for further analysis. Two functions 'DHT11_read()' and 'SD_write()' are created which reads the sensor data and writes it on the SD card repeatedly. The two functions are called at a delay of 3 seconds.

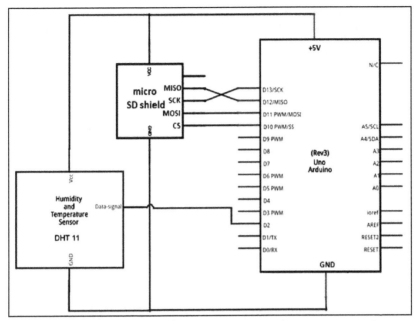

Figure 18.9: Interfacing micro SD card shield and DHT 11 with Arduino board schematic diagram

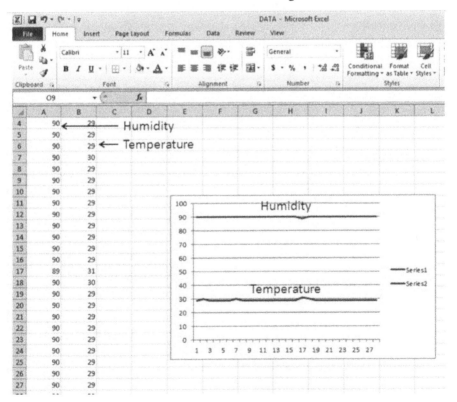

A CSV file 'DATA.csv' is created to store the sensor values with the humidity and temperature values stored in two separate columns. The values in the 'DATA.csv' file can also be plotted to notice their change with time.

Program:

```
#include <dht11.h> //Include DHT11 library
#include <SD.h> // include the SD library

int CS = 10; //initialize chip select pin to 10
File myFile; //create a data file object named 'myFile'

dht11 DHT11; //create DHT11 object
int Humidity, Temperature; //declare variables to store values

void setup()
{
 Serial.begin(9600); //start serial communication
 Serial.println("Initializing the SD card");
 if(!SD.begin(CS)) //start SD card via SPI communication
 {
 Serial.println("Initialization Failed !!!");
 return; //exit from the setup function
 }
 Serial.println("Initialization Completed");

}

void loop()
{
 DHT11_read(); //call function to read the sensor data
 SD_write(); //write the data on the micro SD card shield

 Serial.println("");
 delay(3000); //wait for 3 seconds

}

void SD_write()
{
```

```
 myFile = SD.open("DATA.csv", FILE_WRITE); // open a csv
file 'DATA.csv'

 if(myFile)
 {
 myFile.print(Humidity); //write 'DATA 1' on SD card
 myFile.print(","); //shift to next column
 myFile.println(Temperature); //write 'DATA 2' on SD card
 Serial.println("Writing on SD card Complete"); //prints on
Serial monitor
 myFile.close(); //close and save the text file
 }
 else
 {
 Serial.println("Error in opening the file"); //prints on
Serial monitor
 }


}

void DHT11_read()
{
DHT11.read(2); //read data from digital pin 2

Humidity=DHT11.humidity; //get the value of humidity from
sensor
Temperature=DHT11.temperature; //get the value of temperature
from sensor

Serial.print("Humidity (%): ");
Serial.println(Humidity); //print the value of humidity on
serial monitor

Serial.print("Temperature (°C): ");
Serial.println(Temperature); //print the value of temperature
on serial monitor
}
//end
```

Project 18.6: Reading Temperature and humidity values from SD Card

The following project will demonstrate how to read values from a CSV file stored in a SD card. It uses serial monitor to display the data bytes read from the SD card. A CSV file named 'DATA.csv' is created as shown below.

Explanation:

The program is similar to the one for reading a text file from SD card. The while loop continues to read a byte of data and appends it to a string variable 'Value'. Each row is read at a time. A newline character '\n' signifies the end of reading a complete row. Two column values are separated by a comma.

Each row values are simultaneously printed on the serial monitor.

Program:

```
#include <SD.h> // include the SD library
int CS = 10; //initialize chip select pin to 10

File myFile; //create a data file object named 'myFile'
String Value; //declare string variable 'Value'
void setup()
{
 Serial.begin(9600); //start serial communication
 Serial.println("Initializing the SD card");
 if(!SD.begin(CS)) //start SD card via SPI communication
 {
 Serial.println("Initialization Failed !!!");
 return; //exit from the setup function
 }
Serial.println("Initialization Completed");
}
void loop()
{
 myFile = SD.open("DATA.csv"); // open a csv file 'DATA.csv'


 if(myFile) //if the text file 'DATA.csv' exists
 {
while(myFile.available()) //continue till the data is available
 {
char c = myFile.read(); //read and store the data from file
in character variable 'c'
Value=Value+c; //append the data to string 'Value'
if(c=='\n') //if the data read is a newline character '\n'
 {
Serial.println(Value); //print the string 'Value' on
serial monitor
 Value=""; //clear the string
 }
 }
 myFile.close(); //close and save the text file
```

```
}
else
{
Serial.println("Error in opening the file");
}
delay(3000); //wait for 3 secs
 Serial.println("\n\n\n\n"); //skip four lines on serial
monitor
}
//end
```

Arduino with Matlab

In this Arduino with MATLAB project we will learn how to control the Arduino board using MATLAB GUI (Graphic User Interface). USB COM port is used as the interface standard for serial communication between MATLAB and Arduino board. The serial communication provides an easy and accurate way to control, monitor and collect processed data to and fro the Arduino board. The Arduino board always needs to be connected to the USB port for successful communication during the working of this project.

Serial communication is the simplest way to communicate between two devices. Here information from MATLAB to Arduino is sent in serial fashion i.e. one bit at a time. The transmission begins with start bit (logic 0) and is followed by the string of data bits, starting with least significant bit (LSB) and ending with most significant bit (MSB). The no of bits transferred per second is given by the baud rate. The standard baud rate of 9600 bits/sec will be used for this project.

Project 19.1: LED control through MATLAB GUI

Let us start by making a MATLAB GUI with two buttons for turning ON and OFF a LED on the Arduino board. You need to install MATLAB software to proceed further with the project. MATLAB 2010 is being used for building the GUI and communicating with Arduino board. Once the MATLAB software is installed, open the software and go to Files → New → GUI.

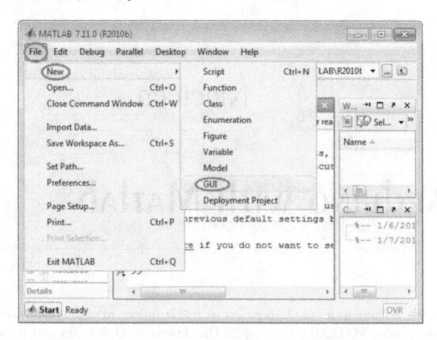

This opens a new window where we need to select 'Blank GUI (Default)'.

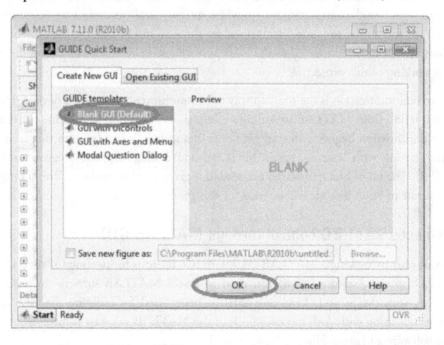

Press OK and a new GUI layout will open up as shown below. Add four 'Push Buttons' from the items on the left side. The 'Push Button' is highlighted and can be placed on the layout by drag and drop option.

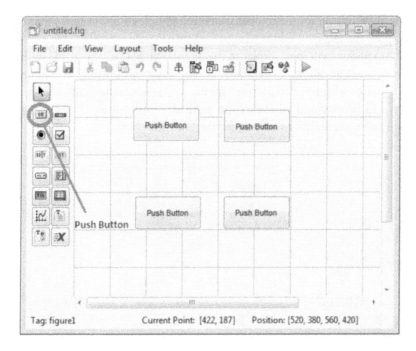

Right click on the first push button and select the 'Property Inspector' option. Here change the 'String' and 'Tag' name to 'START' and 'start' respectively. Similarly change the 'String' and 'Tag' name to 'STOP' and 'stop' for the second push button, 'ON' and 'on' and finally 'OFF' and 'off' for the third and fourth push button respectively. Finally the GUI layout should look similar the one shown below.

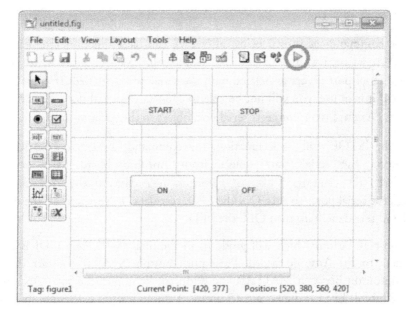

Press the 'play' button on the toolbar which is highlighted in the above figure. Doing this will guide us to a new 'editor window' where programming for GUI is to be done. The editor window will look similar to the one shown below. The m-file in the editor window consists of call back functions for each push button that we had created in the GUI layout with their respective 'tag' name. The commands inside the call back function will be executed whenever the particular push button is pressed. Here we have four call back functions created for the four push buttons.

Add the commands as shown below after each call back function. The command 'Arduino=serial('COM4')' under the 'START' call back function creates a serial port object associated with the serial port specified. If port does not exist, or if it is in use, you will not be able to connect the serial port. The command 'fopen(Arduino)' connects serial port object to the Arduino board.

Under the 'STOP' call back function, the command 'fclose(Arduino)' disconnects the serial port object from Arduino board. The command 'fprintf(Arduino,'text')' writes text data to the Arduino board through the serial port. To turn ON the LED, text data '1' is written on the Arduino board and text data '0' to turn OFF the LED.

Press the play button which will guide us to the final GUI. Final GUI is used to send data to the Arduino board. Press push button 'START' to start the serial communication between MATLAB and Arduino. Press push button 'ON' to turn ON the inbuilt LED at digital pin 13 on the Arduino board i.e. the inbuilt LED on the Arduino board, and press push button 'OFF' to turn the LED OFF. Finally press push button 'STOP' to terminate the serial communication.

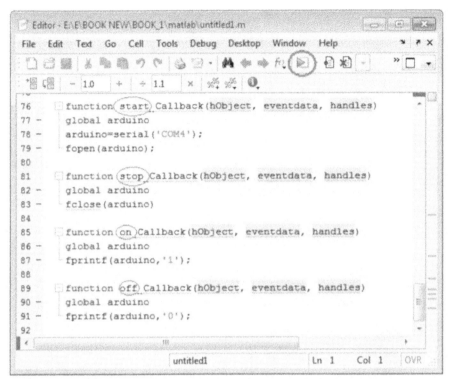

Explanation:

We will be testing on the inbuilt LED connected to digital pin 13 on the Arduino board. Connect the Arduino board to your computer through the USB cable and upload the Arduino sketch to the board. Now you can start controlling the LED from the MATAB GUI.

Whenever we press the push button 'ON' from the GUI, character '1' is received by the microcontroller on the Arduino board. Under this situation the LED at digital pin 13 is turned ON. On pressing 'OFF' push button, character '0' is received and the LED is turned OFF.

Program:

```
int LED = 13;

void setup()
{
```

```
 Serial.begin(9600); //start the serial communication at
baud rate 9600
 pinMode(LED, OUTPUT); // initialize the digital pin as an
output.
}


void loop()
{
 if(Serial.available()>0) //if serial data is received
 {
 char c = Serial.read();

 if(c=='1') //read the serial data
 {          //if serial data received is '1'
 digitalWrite(LED, HIGH); // turn the LED on
 }
 else if(c=='0') //if serial data received is '0'
 {
 digitalWrite(LED, LOW); // turn the LED off
 }


 }
}

//end
```

Project 19.2: Receiving and plotting sensor data in MATLAB GUI

In the above project we succeeded in transferring data from MATAB GUI to Arduino board and perform the task of turning ON and OFF a LED. Similarly we can also send data from Arduino board back to the MATLAB GUI.

The project will be using a photo resistor to sense the intensity of light in a room and plot the same on the MATLAB GUI. Photo resistor changes it resistance with the ambient light in the room, hence they are light sensitive devices. As the light on the photo-resistor increases, its resistance decreases and vice versa. If we hook up the photo-resistor with a fixed resistance in voltage divider circuit, we can essentially feed into the analog input of the Arduino board a voltage that varies with the intensity of light in the room. For more information on photo resistor refer to chapter 4.

So let us start by building the MATLAB GUI. Follow the steps mentioned earlier in the project 19.1 to create a blank GUI. Drag and drop three push buttons and axes to plot the data received from the Arduino.

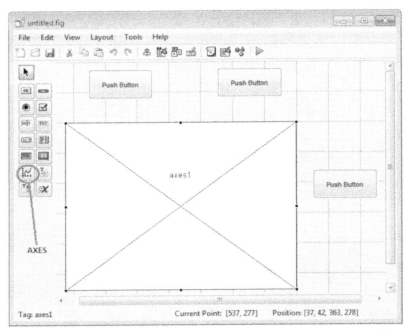

Right click on each push button and go to the property Inspector option. Change the string and tag name of the first push button to 'START' and 'start'. Similarly change the string and tag name to 'STOP', 'stop' and 'PLOT', 'plot' for the second and third push buttons respectively. The final GUI layout would look similar to the one shown below.

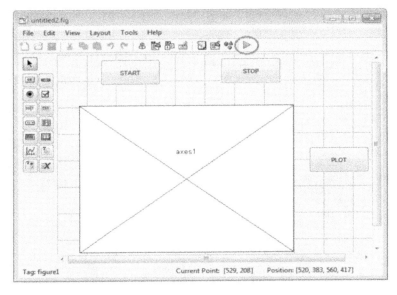

Press on the play button on the tools bar which will guide us to a new editor window. Here a call back function for each push button is automatically created with their tag names.

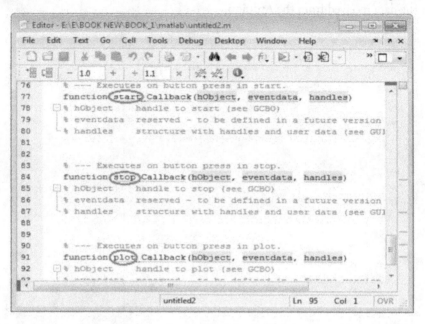

Add the lines as shown below under each call back function.

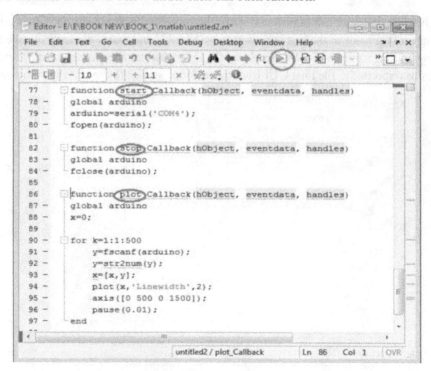

The command lines under the 'start' and 'stop' call back function are similar to the earlier projects in this chapter. Under the 'plot' call back function, we continuously scan and read the text data in variable 'y' for 500 times. The line `y=fscanf(Arduino)'` reads the text data received from the Arduino. The next line `y=str2num(y)` converts the data from text to integer format. After this we plot the received data and also limit the maximum values for x axis and y axis to 500 and 1500 respectively.

Press on the play button on the tools bar and the final GUI will appear. This is the GUI that the user can use to plot the current light intensity of the room.

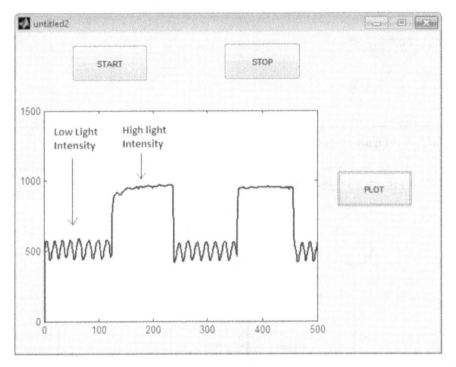

The user should start by pressing on the 'START' push button which initiates the communication between the MATLAB GUI and Arduino board. Then press 'PLOT' push button and the plotting of the light intensity of the room will start. When the intensity of light is low, the values received are approximately around 500. When the light in the room has increased, the values received increases to around 1000. Similarly we can receive data from any kind of sensors through the Arduino board and also plot them for visual reference. Finally the user should close the communication by pressing the 'STOP' push button.

We need to build the following circuit to read the intensity of light. The value is read across the resistor through analog pin 'A0' of Arduino board.

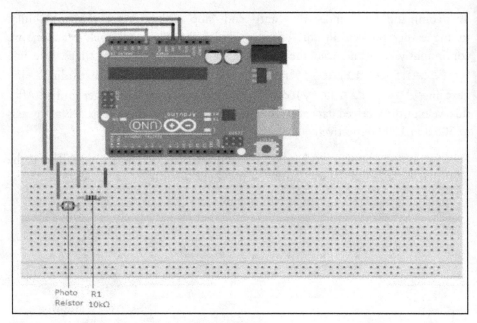

Figure 19.1: Analog input with photo-resistor wiring diagram

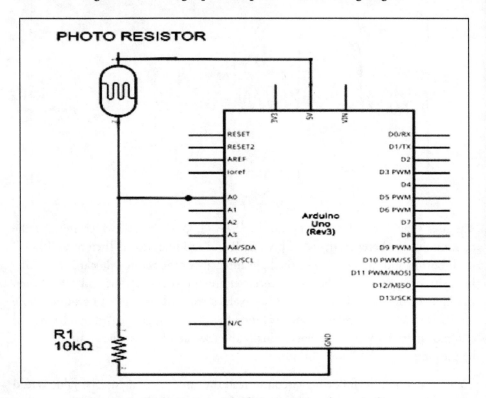

Figure 19.2: Analog input with photo-resistor schematic diagram

Explanation:

Before testing the MATLAB GUI, upload the Arduino program with the necessary circuitry for photo resistor. The program constantly reads the sensor value at analog pin 'A0' and simultaneously prints it to the serial COM port 4. Every time the sensor value is printed, the corresponding value is received by the MATLAB GUI. The value is thereby plotted on the GUI axes.

Program:

```
int sensorPin = A0; // select the input pin for the sensor
int sensorValue = 0; // variable to store the value coming
from the sensor

void setup()
{
Serial.begin(9600); //start communication with MATLAB
}

void loop()
{

  sensorValue = analogRead(sensorPin); // read the value
from the sensor:
  Serial.println(sensorValue); //send the value to MATLAB
  delay(100);
}

//end
```

C hapter Twenty

Real Time Clock

In this project we'll learn how to set the time and date on the RTC (Real Time Clock) module and then retrieve and display it on the Serial Monitor as well as on a LCD display. RTC modules are very useful for time related projects such as temperature data logging, biometric attendance systems, alarm clocks etc.

Figure 20.1 shows a breakout board of a RTC module based on the clock chip DS3231, which supports the I2C protocol. There are older versions of RTC chip such as DS1302 and 1307. The DS3231 is a low-cost, extremely accurate I2C real-time clock (RTC) with an integrated crystal. The device incorporates a battery (CR 2032) input and maintains accurate timekeeping when main power to the device is interrupted.

Figure 20.1: Real-time clock IC module

Components

- Arduino board

- DS3231 RTC module

- LCD 16x2

- Breadboard

Project 20.1: Setting the RTC Module

The RTC maintains seconds, minutes, hours, day, date, month, and year information. The date at the end of the month is automatically adjusted for months with fewer than 31 days, including corrections for leap year. The clock operates in either the 24-hour or 12-hour format with an AM/PM indicator. Address and data are transferred serially through an I2C bidirectional bus.

The following table illustrates the recommended operating conditions for DS3231 RTC module.

Table 20.1: DS3231 RTC module specifications

S.No	Parameter	Symbol	Typical Value
1.	Supply Voltage	Vcc	2.5 - 5.5 V
2.	Battery (LI-Ion)	VBAT	2.5 - 3.5 V
3.	Active Battery Current	IBAT	70-150µA
4.	Logic 1 Input SDA, SCL	VIH	0.7xVcc
5.	Logic 0 Input SDA, SCL	VIL	0.3xVcc

Arduino and DS3231 RTC module communicates through I2C bus. I2C (Inter-Integrated Circuit) bus provides a standard and simple means to control many devices at a time such as real-time clocks, digital potentiometers, digital compasses, LCD displays etc. Each I2C device has a unique address for the Arduino to distinguish one device from the other. The RTC module address byte contains 7-bit data, which is 1101000 (68H). Common I²C bus speeds range from 10 Kbit/s to 400 Kbit/s.

I2C protocol uses two bidirectional lines, Serial Data Line (SDA) and Serial Clock Line (SCL) to establish a proper communication. SDA is the data input/output line for the I2C serial interface and SCL is the clock input for the I2C serial interface and is used to synchronize data movement. In the case of the Arduino Uno, the SDA pin is A4 and the SCL pin is A5, as shown in figure 20.2.

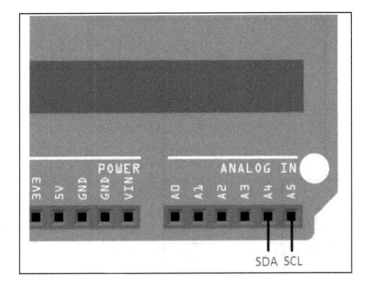

Figure 20.2: I2C bus on Arduino Uno board

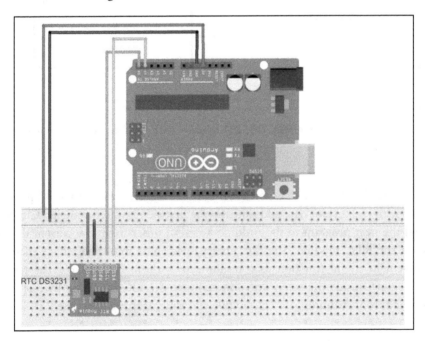

Figure 20.3: Interfacing RTC DS3231 module with Arduino wiring diagram

So now after finishing with the introduction part, let us go for making the actual setup. In the wiring diagram, connect the SDA and SCL pins of DS3231 RTC module to the analog pins A4 and A5 respectively on the Arduino board. The module is powered from the 5V and GND pins of the Arduino.

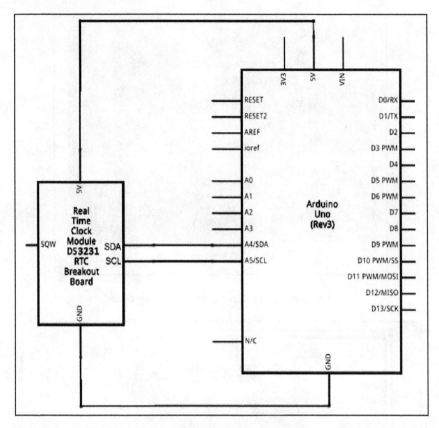

Figure 20.4: Interfacing RTC DS3231 module with Arduino schematic diagram

Explanation:

While using the RTC module for the first time, we need to setup and update the module with the current date and time. So the first step is to setup the RTC module. Upload the next program to the Arduino board in order to set the current date and time on the RTC module. The I2C library 'Wire.h' is imported which enables us to implement useful function to communicate with an I2C device. The function 'Wire.begin()' inside the setup function activates the I2C bus. One byte of data is transferred from Arduino to RTC module at a time, starting from the RTC module address i.e. 68H

Another user-defined function 'set()' is called to write the current date and time on the RTC module register. After each byte is received, an acknowledgement bit is transmitted from RTC module to Arduino. The module is set for 0 seconds, 4 minutes, 2 pm, Thursday, 5th of November 2015.

Once the 'set()' function is called, the process of setting the module with current date and time requires the following three functions.

1. Arduino generates the START condition by sending the address of the RTC module i.e. 68H.

   The Wire.beginTransmission(DS3231_ADDRESS);

2. The next function writes a byte of data in a sequence starting from second, minute, hour, dayOfWeek, dayOfMonth, month and year.

   Wire.write(data);

3. Finally once we finish with sending the data, we need to end the process of data transmission with the following function.

Wire.endTransmission();

Lastly a custom function 'decToBcd(byte val)' is created to convert the decimal numbers to BCD values because the DS3231 RTC module stores value in BCD format.

Program:

```
#include <Wire.h>
#define DS3231_ADDRESS 0x68

void setup()
{
Wire.begin();

// seconds, minutes, hours, day, date, month, year
set(0, 4, 14, 5, 5, 11, 15);
}
```

```
void set(byte second, byte minute, byte hour, byte dayOfWeek,
byte dayOfMonth, byte month, byte year)
{
// sets time and date data to DS3231

Wire.beginTransmission(DS3231_ADDRESS);
Wire.write(0); //set DS3232 register pointer to 00h
Wire.write(decToBcd(second)); // set seconds
Wire.write(decToBcd(minute)); // set minutes
Wire.write(decToBcd(hour));  // set hours
Wire.write(decToBcd(dayOfWeek)); // set day of week
(1=Sunday, 7=Saturday)
Wire.write(decToBcd(dayOfMonth)); // set date (1 to 31)
Wire.write(decToBcd(month)); // set month
Wire.write(decToBcd(year)); // set year (0 to 99)
Wire.endTransmission();
}


// function to convert normal decimal numbers to binary
coded decimal

byte decToBcd(byte val)
{
return( (val/10*16) + (val%10) );
}

void loop()
{

}
//end
```

Project 20.2: Reading current date and time from the RTC Module

Now after setting the RTC module, we would like to see the result on the serial monitor. The next program helps the Arduino to read the current date and time from the appropriate register bytes. The DS3231 timekeeping registers holds the values of seconds, minutes, hours, day, date, month, year from address 00H to 06H.

Table 20.2: Address mapping of Timekeeping registers

S.No	Address	Function	Range
1.	00H	Seconds	00-59
2.	01H	Minutes	00-59
3.	02H	Hours	00-23
4.	03H	Day	1-7
5.	04H	Date	01-31
6.	05H	Month	01-12
7.	06H	Year	00-99

Explanation:

Arduino initiates the communication with DS3231 and requests for 7 bytes of data starting from address 00H. The first byte is seconds, followed by minutes and so on up to the year value. Data are transferred with the most significant bit (MSB) first. Arduino generates all the serial clock pulses and the START and STOP conditions.

Two custom functions 'read_DS3231()' and 'displayTime()' are used to read date and time values and display them on the serial monitor respectively. BCD value is read from DS3231 registers, therefore BCD to decimal conversion needs to be performed before displaying the value on the serial monitor. Serial monitor is updated every second. The result on the serial monitor should look similar as shown below.

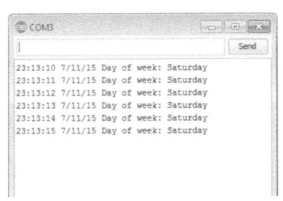

Program:

```
#include <Wire.h>
#define DS3231_ADDRESS 0x68

//initialize variables
int second, minute, hour, dayOfWeek, dayOfMonth, month, year;
```

```
void setup()
{
Wire.begin();
Serial.begin(9600); //start serial communication
}


void read_DS3231() //function to read date and time
{
Wire.beginTransmission(DS3231_ADDRESS);
Wire.write(0); // set DS3232 register pointer to 00h
Wire.requestFrom(DS3231_ADDRESS, 7); // request seven bytes
of data starting from register 00h

second = bcdToDec(Wire.read()); //read seconds
minute = bcdToDec(Wire.read()); //read minutes
hour = bcdToDec(Wire.read()); //read hours
dayOfWeek = bcdToDec(Wire.read()); //read day of week
(1=Sunday, 7=Saturday)
dayOfMonth = bcdToDec(Wire.read()); //read date (1 to 31)
month = bcdToDec(Wire.read()); //read month
year = bcdToDec(Wire.read()); //read year (0 to 99)
Wire.endTransmission();


}

void displayTime()
{

// retrieve data from DS3232
read_DS3231();

// print it to the serial monitor
Serial.print(hour); // convert the byte variable to a
decimal number before displaying
Serial.print(":");
Serial.print(minute);
Serial.print(":");
```

```
Serial.print(second);
Serial.print(" ");
Serial.print(dayOfMonth);
Serial.print("/");
Serial.print(month);
Serial.print("/");
Serial.print(year);
Serial.print(" Day of week: ");
switch(dayOfWeek){
case 1:
Serial.println("Sunday");
break;
case 2:
Serial.println("Monday");
break;
case 3:
Serial.println("Tuesday");
break;
case 4:
Serial.println("Wednesday");
break;
case 5:
Serial.println("Thursday");
break;
case 6:
Serial.println("Friday");
break;
case 7:
Serial.println("Saturday");
break;
}
}

// Convert binary coded decimal to normal decimal numbers
int bcdToDec(byte val)
{
return( (val/16*10) + (val%16) );
```

```
}

void loop()
{
displayTime(); // display the real-time clock data on the
Serial Monitor,
delay(1000); // every second
}

//end
```

Project 20.3: Displaying current date and time on 16x2 LCD

Further we can display the values of date and time on a character 16x2 LCD display. We'll be using libraries and functions from previous program along with the codes from Project 9. Digital pins 2, 4, 8, 9, 10 and 11 of Arduino are used to interface with LCD display.

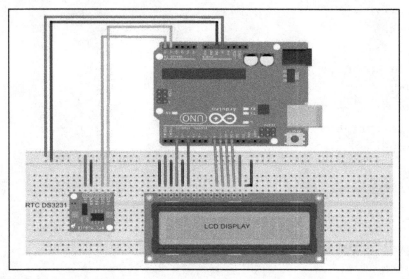

Figure 20.5: Interfacing RTC DS3231 and LCD with Arduino wiring diagram

Explanation:

Instead of printing the values on the serial monitor, the current date and time needs to appear on the LCD display. Hence compared to earlier sketch from Project 20.2, the command 'serial.print' is replaced with 'lcd.print' inside function 'displayTime()'. The LCD display is cleared and updated every second.

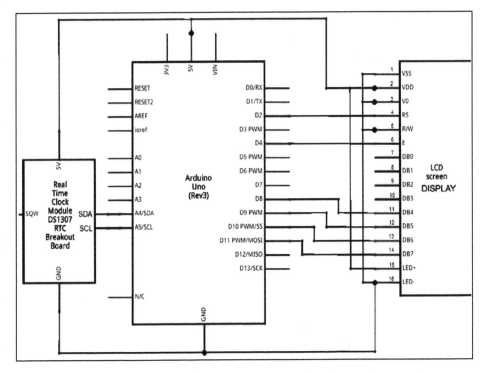

Figure 20.6: Interfacing RTC DS3231 and LCD with Arduino schematic diagram

Upload the sketch and the result should be similar to the one shown below.

Program:

```
#include <Wire.h>
#include <LiquidCrystal.h>

#define DS3231_ADDRESS 0x68

//initialize variables
int second, minute, hour, dayOfWeek, dayOfMonth, month,
year;
// initialize the library with the numbers of the interface pins
LiquidCrystal lcd(2, 4, 8, 9, 10, 11); //RS, Enable, D4,
D5, D6, D7
```

```
void setup()
{
Wire.begin();
lcd.begin(16, 2);// set up the LCD's number of columns and
rows
}


void read_DS3231() //function to read date and time
{
Wire.beginTransmission(DS3231_ADDRESS);
Wire.write(0); // set DS3231 register pointer to 00h
Wire.requestFrom(DS3231_ADDRESS, 7); // request seven bytes
of data starting from register 00h

second = bcdToDec(Wire.read()); //read seconds
minute = bcdToDec(Wire.read()); //read minutes
hour = bcdToDec(Wire.read());//read hours
dayOfWeek = bcdToDec(Wire.read()); //read   day   of   week
(1=Sunday, 7=Saturday)
dayOfMonth = bcdToDec(Wire.read()); //read date (1 to 31)
month = bcdToDec(Wire.read()); //read month
year = bcdToDec(Wire.read()); //read year (0 to 99)
Wire.endTransmission();
}

int bcdToDec(byte val) // Convert binary coded decimal to
normal decimal numbers
{
return( (val/16)*10 + (val%16) );
}

void displayTime()
{

read_DS3231();

lcd.print(dayOfMonth);
lcd.print('/');
lcd.print(month);
```

```
lcd.print('/');
lcd.print(year);
lcd.print(' ');
lcd.print(hour);
lcd.print(':');
lcd.print(minute);
lcd.print(':');
lcd.print(second);

lcd.setCursor(0, 1); //set cursor of lcd to column 0, line 1

switch(dayOfWeek){
case 1:
lcd.print("Sunday");
break;
case 2:
lcd.print("Monday");
break;
case 3:
lcd.print("Tuesday");
break;
case 4:
lcd.print("Wednesday");
break;
case 5:
lcd.print("Thursday");
break;
case 6:
lcd.print("Friday");
break;
case 7:
lcd.print("Saturday");
break;
}
}

void loop()
{
```

```
lcd.clear(); //clear lcd display
lcd.setCursor(0, 0); //set cursor of lcd to column 0, line 0
displayTime(); // display the real-time clock data on the
lcd
delay(1000); // wait for a second
}

//end
```

INVERTER USING MOSFET

This project shows how to build an inverter using N and P-type MOSFET. The project aims to efficiently covert DC power to a high voltage AC source, so that it can be used to charge laptops, lighting, run fans and other domestic appliances. The work of converting DC power to AC can be achieved using power transistor, MOSFET or Thyristor. Inverters come in all shapes and sizes, from low power functions such as powering a radio or charging cell phones in a car to that of lighting up a building in case of power outage.

Components

- Arduino board

- N channel MOSFETs (IRF 540N)

- P channel MOSFETs (IRF 9540N)

- Battery (12V, 3A)

- Incandescent Lamp (20W, AC load)

- Transformer (12V/230V, 3A)

- Transistor (2N2222)

- Resistance (1kΩ)

- Breadboard

Project 21.1: Inverter design using MOSFET's

The device which converts DC power to AC power is termed as 'inverter' derived from the word 'inversion'. The process of inversion can be achieved in two ways. The DC power can be stepped up using a DC-DC boost converter and followed by conversion of high voltage DC power to high voltage AC power at 50Hz frequency. Another way is to initially convert low voltage DC power to AC and then use a transformer to step up the voltage to approximately 230V for domestic use.

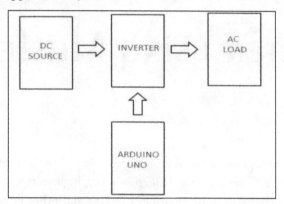

Figure 21.1: Signal flow diagram for a complete inverter circuit

The DC sources can be made available using batteries, solar panels or by using DC generators. There is range of battery voltages available in the market and the standard ones being 6V, 9V, 12V, 24V and so on.

There are two types of inverters available in the market with modified sine wave (MSW) output and pure sine wave output also known as true sine wave (TSW) inverter. In a modified sine wave, the voltage rises and continues to remain positive for a fixed time and falls abruptly to maintain a constant negative potential across the load as per the required load frequency. Pure Sine Wave inverters supply power similar to what we receive at the wall outlets. Pure sine wave inverters are used to operate sensitive electronic devices that require high quality waveform with little harmonic distortion

The choice of MSW or TSW depends on the load on the AC side. If the need is to drive an inductive load such as induction motor or to power up a resistive load like an incandescent lamp, MSW is more economical compared to TSW inverter. Also, the modified sine wave is a form of square wave, alternating and changing polarities every 10msec to achieve a frequency of 50Hz which contains odd harmonics. With a fundamental frequency of 50Hz, there will be 3rd odd harmonics of 150Hz, 5th harmonic of 250 Hz and so on. These harmonic contents in a modified sine wave causes over heating of motors and introduces electrical noise in fluorescent lights, audio amplifiers and TV monitors. This disadvantage of MSW prevents it from supplying certain loads like laser printers, coffee maker and digital clock which uses AC current to calculate time for their processor operation. The processor timing depends on the time interval between the consecutive zero crossing of the AC current. TSW crosses zero clearly, but MSW signal takes few milli seconds to cross zero and result in improper operation of the processor because of multiple zero detections. Figure 21.2 shows the waveforms for a pure and modified sine wave. The modified sine waveform is easy to produce because the switching needs to be done between 3 values at set frequencies of 50Hz. The turn-on time (period for which the waveform is positive) and turn-off time (period for which the waveform is negative) of MSW can be adjusted at 50Hz frequency. The turn-on time and turn-off is regulated using Arduino Uno. Arduino Uno also helps us to vary the frequency of the AC output and also to set the output AC frequency at any desirable value.

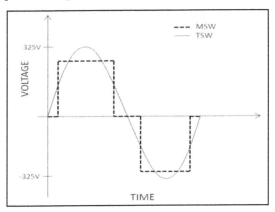

Figure 21.2: Modified sine wave and True sine wave

TSW inverters are highly reliable and do not produce electrical noise those associated with MSW inverters. Pulse Width Modulation (PWM) technique is used to produce pure sine waves for powering up digitally operated devices and other calibrated measuring equipment's. To start with the basic operation and understand the working of an inverter, the project deals with the building of MSW inverter to drive a 20W incandescent lamp.

Important device that is used for switching purpose in this project is a semiconductor device called MOSFET. MOSFET (Metal Oxide Semiconductor Field Effect Transistor) is a voltage controlled field effect transistor and has a metal oxide Gate electrode which is electrically insulated from the main semiconductor n-channel or p-channel by a very thin layer of insulating material usually silicon dioxide. Due to the insulating material between the Gate and the semiconductor surface, typically no significant gate current flows in either ON or OFF state.

It is a three terminal device and can be used both as a switch or an amplifier. It is a Unipolar device i.e. there is only one charge carrier either holes or electrons.

Since 1970's MOSFET (Metal Oxide Semiconductor Field Effect Transistor) became very popular mostly because of its high switching speed above 500 kHz. Most VLSI circuits made at present are using MOS technology.

The basic types of MOSFETs available are:

1. **Depletion Type:** The transistor requires the Gate-Source voltage, (VGS) to switch the device "OFF". The depletion mode MOSFET is equivalent to a "Normally Closed" switch. Also there is presence of physical channel in the substrate.

2. **Enhancement Type:** The transistor requires a Gate-Source voltage, (VGS) to switch the device "ON". The enhancement mode MOSFET is equivalent to a "Normally Open" switch. Physical channel is absent in case of Enhancement MOSFET.

Figure 21.3 illustrates the basic structure of depletion type n-channel and p-channel MOSFET. Drain and source are connected by a physical channel which makes the device normally switched ON without the application of gate bias voltage.

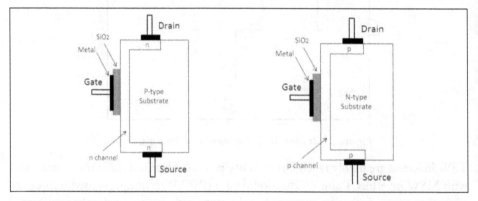

Figure 21.3: Basic structure of Depletion type MOSFET a) N-channel b) P-channel

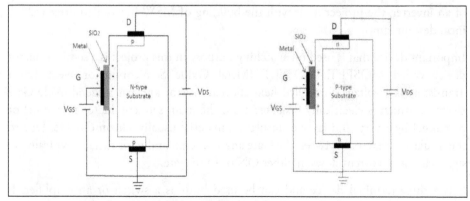

Figure 21.4: Operation of Depletion type MOSFET a) N-channel b) P-channel

For the n-channel depletion MOSFET, a negative gate-source voltage (-VGS) will deplete the n-channel from its free electrons thereby switching the transistor OFF. Negative gate-source voltage will introduce more positive ions in the physical n-channel and restricts the flow of current from drain to source. Likewise for p-channel depletion MOSFET a positive gate-source voltage (+VGS) will deplete the channel of its free holes and therefore turning it OFF.

Enhancement type MOSFET transistor has no physical channel which means the device is normally switched OFF. Both n-channel and p-channel are shown in the figure 21.5.

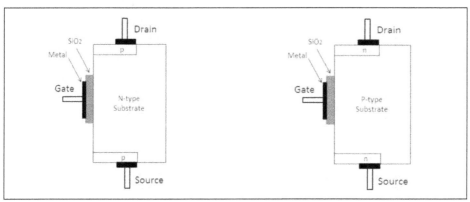

Figure 21.5: Basic structure of Enhancement type MOSFET a) N-channel b) P-channel

For the n-channel enhancement MOSET, a drain current will only flow when a positive gate voltage (VGS) is applied to the gate terminal. The application of a positive gate-source voltage will create a layer of negative charges near the SiO2 insulation layer of the gate. This enhances the thickness of the channel allowing more current to flow from drain to gate.

Increasing this positive gate voltage will cause the channel resistance to decrease further causing an increase in the drain current through the channel.

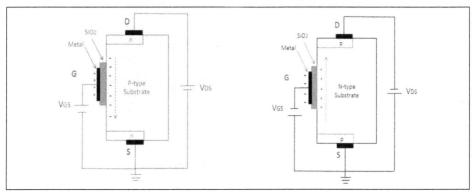

Figure 21.6: Operation of Enhancement type MOSFET a) N-channel b) P-channel

Negative gate-source voltage is required to turn ON the p-channel enhancement MOSFET. The application of a negative gate-source voltage causes positive ions to form a channel for the flow of current from source to drain. Increasing the negative gate voltage enhances the conductivity of the channel.

The schematic symbols for the n-channel and p-channel enhancement and depletion type MOSFETs are shown in figure 21.7. The broken lines in case of enhancement type MOSFET symbolize the absence of physical channel.

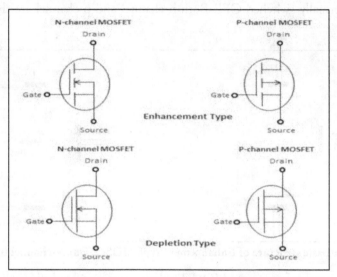

Figure 21.7: Symbols for Enhancement and Depletion type n and p-channel MOSFETs

In this project we are using IRF540N n-channel MOSFET and IRF9540N p-channel MOSFET to build an inverter. For IRF540N n-channel MOSFET a positive gate voltage turns ON the transistor and with zero or negative gate voltage, the transistor will be OFF. For IRF9540N p-channel MOSFET, zero or negative gate voltage will turn ON the transistor and with positive gate voltage, the transistor will be OFF.

Table 21.1: Switching conditions for IRF540N and IRF9540N

Enhancement MOSFET	VGS = +ve	VGS = 0	VGS = -ve
IRF540N n-channel	ON	OFF	OFF
IRF9540N p-channel	OFF	ON	ON

One of the ways to design an inverter is to build a basic H bridge circuit. An H bridge circuit can be build using relays, transistors or MOSFETs to operate as switching element in the circuit. The circuit consists of four switches S1 to S4 as shown in figure 21.8. The switches are turned ON and OFF in pairs for controlling the direction of current flow through the load.

Table 21.2: Absolute Ratings of IRF540N and IRF9540N

Parameters	IRF540N	IRF9540N
1. Drain to Source voltage (VDS)	100V	-100V
2. Drain current (ID)	33A	-23A
3. Gate-to-Source voltage	±20V	±20V
4. Drain to Source Resistance (RDS) - (On condition)	0.044Ω	0.117Ω

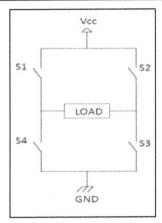

Figure 21.8: Basic H bridge circuit with four switches

As shown in the figure 21.9 (a), if switch S1 and S3 are closed then the left lead of the load gets connected to the positive terminal of the supply and the current flows through switch S1, from left to right of the load and finally to ground through switch S3. In figure 21.9 (b), if switch S2 and S4 are closed then the direction of current through the load is from right to left. This means by using semiconductor devices such as MOSFET's and turning them ON in sequential pairs we can yield alternating current across the load.

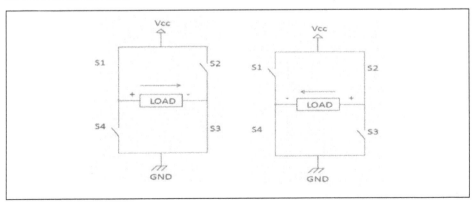

Figure 21.9: H bridge circuit with a) S1 and S3 ON b) S2 and S4 ON

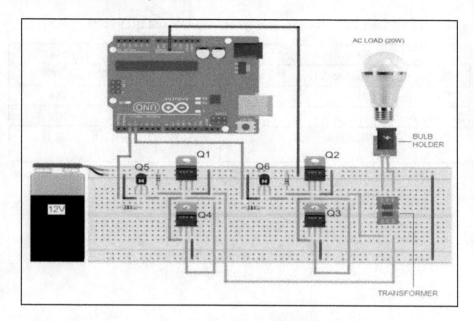

Figure 21.10: Inverter using MOSFET with AC load wiring diagram

Here we shall replace S1 and S2 with IRF9540N and S3 and S4 with IRF540N in order to control the switching using Arduino board. L298 or L293D h bridge IC's can also be used to build a low power inverter.

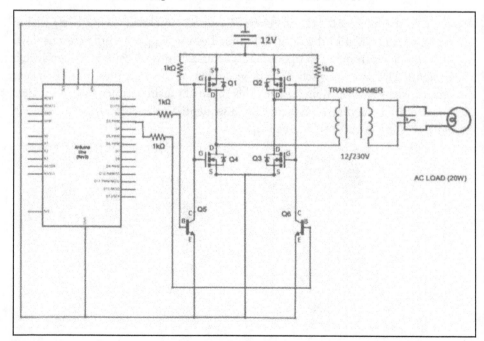

Figure 21.11: Inverter using MOSFET with AC load schematic diagram

Table 21.3: List of transistors used

S.No	Transistor	Specification
1.	Q1, Q2	p-channel (IRF9540N) MOSFETs
2.	Q3, Q4	n-channel (IRF540N) MOSFETs
3.	Q5, Q6	NPN Bipolar Junction Transistor (2N2222)

Explanation:

As discussed earlier, here we are connecting MOSFET's in H-bridge configuration to build an inverter. Here the power rating of the transformer and the 12V DC power supply must be equal or greater than that of the load. The load of 20W is connected to the high voltage side of the transformer.

Q1, Q2 are p-channel (IRF9540N) MOSFET and Q3, Q4 are n-channel (IRF540N) MOSFET. To produce alternating voltage across the primary winding of the transformer, the MOSFET's has to be sequentially turned ON and OFF in pairs. When Q1 and Q3 are turned ON, current starts flowing in the primary winding of the transformer. The direction of the primary current is reversed by switching on the MOSFET pair Q2 and Q4. Thereby we obtain an alternating secondary voltage across the load.

The timely switching of the MOSFET pairs is controlled by Arduino through digital pins '2' and '3'. Digital pin '2' and '3' are switched ON and OFF alternately at a delay of 10 milli seconds. Therefore one cycle is completed in 20 milli seconds i.e. frequency of 50Hz

Initially let us assume all the transistors are OFF and digital pins '2' is set HIGH to +5V. A high voltage at the base of transistor Q5 turns it on, thereby connecting the gate terminals of Q1 and Q4 to ground. Negative gate voltage turns on Q1 (p-channel MOSFET) and simultaneously turns OFF Q4 (n-channel MOSFET). At the same time digital pin '6' is set LOW which keeps transistor Q6 in off condition. This means the gate terminals of Q2 and Q3 directly gets connected to the positive terminal of the battery (+12V). A positive gate voltage turns ON Q3 (n-channel MOSFET) and turns OFF Q2 (p-channel MOSFET).

Similarly on setting digital pin '3' HIGH and digital pin '2' LOW, transistor Q2 and Q4 is turned ON. For 1 milli seconds the output at both the digital pins is LOW (0V). During this time the output voltage is zero since only the lower half transistors (Q4 & Q3) conducts.

In this project instead of using 2N2222 transistor, opto-couplers such as 4N35 can also be used.

Program:

```
void setup() {
// initialize the digital pin as an output.
pinMode(2, OUTPUT);
pinMode(3, OUTPUT);
}
void loop()
{
digitalWrite(2, HIGH);
digitalWrite(3, LOW);
delay(9);
digitalWrite(2, LOW);
digitalWrite(3, LOW);
delay(1);
digitalWrite(2, LOW);
digitalWrite(3, HIGH);
delay(9);
digitalWrite(2, LOW);
digitalWrite(3, LOW);
delay(1);
}
//end
```

AC Regulation and Control

In this project, you'll learn to control and also regulate the mains ac supply of 230V, 50 Hz. This is the voltage which we use in our house for domestic applications. Earlier, the devices used for these applications were auto transformer, resistive potentiometers etc. But due to high efficiency and compact size, Triac ac regulators are used for the purpose of ac regulation and control. The important applications where ac voltage controllers are widely used are speed control of induction motors, lighting control, domestic heating, fan regulators etc.

Before understanding the construction and operation of Triac, let us firstly become familiar with the SCR (Silicon Controlled Rectifier) or commonly known as Thyristor.

Components

- Arduino board
- Triac (BT136)
- MOC 3023
- Resistance (1kΩ)
- Incandescent Lamp (100W, AC load)
- Potentiometer (500kΩ)
- Breadboard

Project 22.1: Switching control of AC load using Triac

A Thyristor is a four layered PNPN switching device, having three junctions J1, J2 and J3. It is a three terminal device namely, the anode (A), cathode (K) and gate (G). The device is always connected in series to the circuit and the gate signal is applied with respect to cathode. The gate terminal is provided at the P2 layer near the cathode.

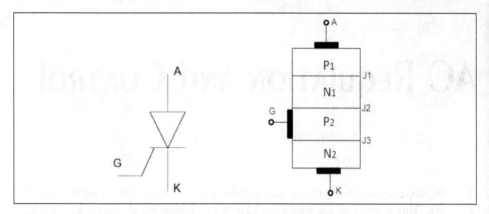

Figure 22.1: Thyristor (a) Structure (b) Symbol

The N2 layer is very thin and highly doped whereas N1 layer is thicker and lightly doped. P1 and P2 layer are thicker and lightly doped compared to N2 layer.

When anode is made positive with respect to the cathode i.e. (VAK), junctions J1 and J3 are forward biased and junction J2 remains reverse biased. Under this condition very small anode current (IA) flows through the device.

When the gate terminal is kept open, the device goes into forward conduction mode when the forward voltage applied (VAK) is equal to the forward breakdown voltage (VBF). The region AB of the characteristic shows that as the device goes into conduction mode, the voltage across the device reduces. Subsequently, the anode current increases and now its value is decided by the load connected in the circuit.

When a positive gate signal is applied, the Thyristor turns ON for a forward voltage (VAK) less than breakdown voltage (VBF). This is because the gate current reduces the depletion layer around J2 by injecting enough electrons in the P2 layer. This increases the concentration of electrons in the P2 layer and thereby reduces the reverse blocking capability of junction J2. Therefore the device turns ON for a smaller value of forward voltage (VAK). Which means the forward voltage at which the device turns ON depends upon the magnitude of gate current i.e. higher the gate current, lower is the forward breakdown voltage.

The value of device current (IA) after which the device goes into conduction mode is called the latching current (IL). Once the device starts conducting, the gate has no control on the device i.e. turning OFF the device is not possible through gate terminal. To turn ON the device it is necessary to keep the gate signal positive unless the value of device current is greater than latching current. After device conducts, it is advantageous to remove the gate signal and make (IG) equal to zero in order to avoid dissipation in the junction.

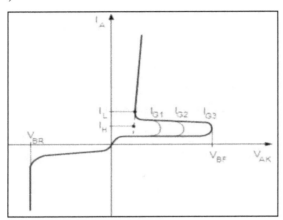

Figure 22.2: V-I characteristics of a Thyristor

Now to turn OFF the device, the anode current which is flowing through the device must be less than the holding current (IH). The process to turn OFF the Thyristor is termed as 'Commutation'. The two methods by which a Thyristor can be commutated are Natural Commutation and Forced Commutation. Only Natural Commutation is used for this project because of its simplicity and wide use. Natural Commutation is achieved in ac circuits where the circuit current passes through zero every half cycle. As the device is connected in series, the anode current becomes less than holding current every half cycle and the device turns OFF.

When anode is made negative with respect to the cathode i.e. (-VAK), junctions J1 and J3 are reverse biased and junction J2 is forward biased. As N2 layer is highly doped and thin, the reverse voltage that junction J3 can block is very small. Therefore junction J1 is responsible to block the entire reverse voltage. The reverse breakdown voltage (VBR) is an indication of breakdown voltage of junction J1.

Thyristor is a unilateral device as the control of power flow from supply to load is possible only in positive half and the device turns off in the negative half. To control the power flow in both halves of the waveform, two Thyristors are connected in inverse parallel where the gates are connected together to form a single device called

Triac. A Triac is a power semiconductor device with three terminals namely T1, T2 and Gate (G).

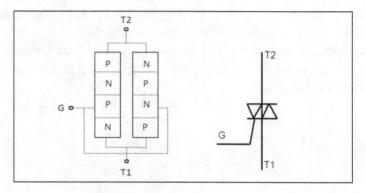

Figure 22.3: Triac (a) Structure (b) Symbol

Figure 22.4: Triac pin diagram

It can conduct current in both the directions (bidirectional) which makes Triac very convenient to be used as switches and regulators for alternating current circuits. Also allowing them to control and regulate very large power with a very low value of gate current. Triac BT136 is used for this project for which the pin configuration is shown below.

The technical specifications for BT136 are listed below.

Table 22.1: BT136 Specifications

S.No	Parameter	Symbol	Maximum Value
1.	Off state voltage	VT	600V
2.	Load Current	I	4A
3.	Gate current	IG	2A
4.	Latching current(VT=12V)	IL	20mA
5.	Holding current (VT=12V)	IH	15mA

To control the switching of lamp load with Arduino, opto-isolators MOC 3023 is also used in the project. An opto-isolator (also known as opto-coupler) is a semiconductor device which uses light to transfer an electrical signal yet remain electrically isolated. MOC 3023 is available in 6 pin DIP and are mostly used as Triac drivers.

Figure 22.5: MOC 3023 pin diagram

Referring to figure 22.5, infrared light emitting diode (LED) is used for signal transmission in the input side and the output side consists of a Silicon Bilateral Switch (SBS). Initially the output terminals 4 and 6 are open. When pin1 is made HIGH (+5V) with respect to pin 2, current starts flowing through infrared LED. In the process, light waves travels through an optical channel and falls on SBS and closes pin 4 and 6.

Table 22.2: Maximum ratings of MOC 3023

Infrared Emitting Diode		
Parameter	Symbol	Value
Reverse Voltage	VR	3V
Forward Current	IF	60mA
Total Power Dissipation	PD	1.33mW
Output Driver		
Off–State Output Terminal Voltage	VOFF	400V
Peak Current	IP	1A
Total Power Dissipation	PD	300mW
Isolation Voltage	VISO	5000V

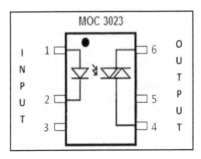

Figure 22.6: MOC 3023 pin diagram

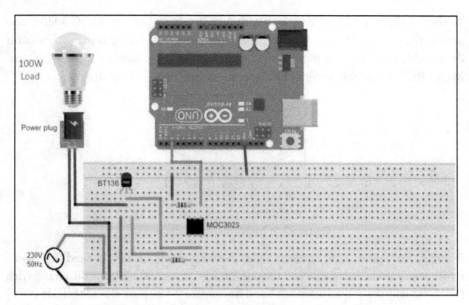

Figure 22.7: Triac switching circuit with AC load wiring diagram

The input pin 1 can easily be controlled using any of the available digital pins on the Arduino board and thereby controlling the switching of the ac circuit connected on the output side of the opto-isolator. A relay could also have been used for the purpose.

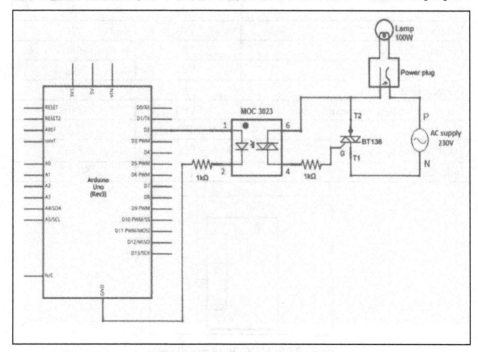

Figure 22.8: Triac switching circuit with AC load schematic diagram

Explanation:

The voltage applied across the device Triac BT136 is alternating and depends upon the AC supply to which the device is connected. Since an AC supply produces alternating voltage, the device is subjected to positive voltage for half a cycle and negative voltage for next half cycle. For the project, the gate terminal is connected to terminal T2 through a resistance, which means the potential of gate G and terminal T2 are same at any instant of time.

With reference to figure 22.8, during positive half cycle let us consider phase terminal 'P' is positive and neutral terminal 'N' is negative. Which means according to the schematic diagram terminal T2 will be positive and terminal T1 negative. The gate terminal being at higher potential than terminal T1, gate current flows from gate to the terminal T1. The P2 layer is flooded with electrons and current starts flowing across P2-N2 junction. This process of recombination breaks down the reverse biased junction between N1 and P2 layers and thereby the device conducts.

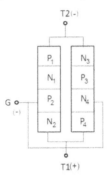

During the negative half cycle, terminal T2 is negative and terminal T1 is positive. The gate terminal being at lower potential than terminal T1, gate current deposits negative charges into the N4 layer. The charges of P3 and N4 layers start recombining and current flows across the P3 and N4 junction. Hence, Triac conducts through P4 N4 P3 N3 layers.

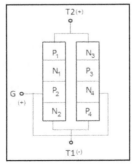

Figure 22.9: Working of Triac during (a) Positive half cycle (b) Negative half cycle

Firstly, let us learn to control the switching of AC load using digital pin 2 of Arduino board. Opto-isolator MOC 3023 is used to trigger Triac BT136. Opto-isolator MOC 3023 make's and break's the connection between gate terminal and terminal T2. Current limiting resistors are used in both the input and output sides of MOC 3023. The opto-isolator also provides isolation between high voltage and low voltage and acts as a protecting device for Arduino board.

Digital pin 2 of Arduino controls the switching of AC load of 100W and is connected to pin 1 of MOC 3023. When digital pin 2 is HIGH, the lamp load is switched ON and on setting digital pin 2 LOW, the lamp load is switched OFF. If we bypass the MOC 3023 and short MOC terminals 4 and 6, the lamp load will always remain ON.

Program:

```
void setup()
{
 pinMode(2, OUTPUT);              // initialize the digital
pin 2 as an output.
}
 void loop()
 {
 digitalWrite(2, HIGH);                  // turn the AC load ON
 delay(1000);              // wait for a second
 digitalWrite(2, LOW);          // turn the AC load OFF
 delay(1000);              // wait for a second
 }
//end
```

Project 22.2: Voltage regulation across AC load using Triac

In addition to switching control, it also equally important to regulate AC power using electronic components. Doing this we can achieve speed control of AC motors and luminescence control of lamp loads. Figure 22.10 illustrates the circuit diagram of the simplest manually controlled lamp dimmer or fan regulator. Nowadays, mostly electronic fan regulators are preferred over conventional fan regulators because of its compact size and higher efficiency. Conventional fan regulators use tapped resistances connected in series due to which most of the energy is lost as heat energy.

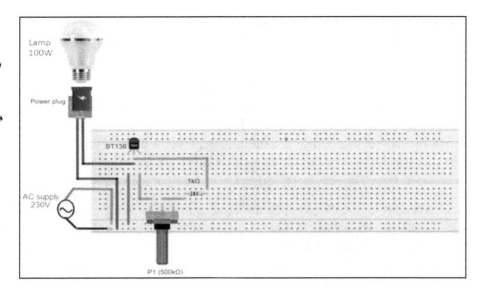

Figure 22.10: Triac regulating circuit with AC load wiring diagram

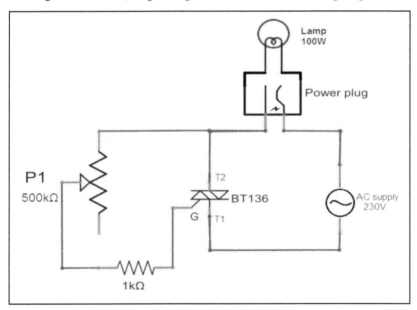

Figure 22.11: Triac regulating circuit with AC load schematic diagram

Explanation:

Triac-based lamp dimmer circuit is designed for controlling the illumination of 100W incandescent lamp. The luminescence of the lamp can be controlled by changing the setting of potentiometer P1. The setting of P1 determines the phase of the gate trigger pulse that triggers the Triac. In other words, by varying P1 we will be able to control the conduction time of Triac and thereby control the lamp load voltage. By varying P1 the load voltage can be controlled from zero to 100%. This project doesn't use an Arduino board.

The gate current decides at which value of terminal voltage VT (across T1 and T2) the Triac conducts. Higher value of terminal voltage VT is required for low value of gate current for the Triac to turn ON and vice versa. The position of potentiometer controls the value of gate current and the firing angle of the device. Firing angle is the angle after which the device conducts measured after the zero crossing. Firing angle can be varied from 0 degrees to 180 degrees in each half of the load voltage.

For a certain setting of P1 (say R1), the Triac turns ON at firing angle θ1. From figure 22.12 when the voltage changes from positive to negative, the Triac turns OFF at zero crossing because the device current becomes less than the holding current. Therefore the conduction time of the device is from θ1 to π for positive half cycle. The load voltage waveform is nearly the same in the negative half.

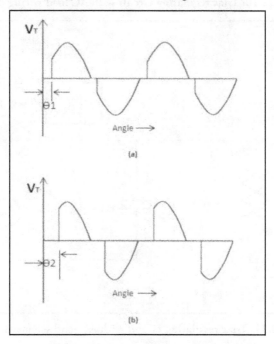

**Figure 22.12: Load voltage waveform a) for setting of potentiometer at R1
b) for setting of potentiometer at R2**

The average voltage Vavg decides the power supplied to the load. It can be computed as:

$$\mathrm{Vavg} = \frac{1}{\pi} \int_0^\pi \mathrm{dt}$$

Since the device conducts from $\theta1$ to π,

$$Vavg = \frac{1}{\pi} \int_{\pi1}^{\pi} dt$$

$$= \frac{Vm}{\pi} [- \cos \omega t]_{\theta1}^{\pi}$$

$$= \frac{Vm}{\pi} [1 + \cos \theta1]$$

Thus, by varying the firing angle $\theta1$ from 0 to π, the average output voltage can be controlled from average voltage $\frac{2Vm}{\pi}$ to zero respectively.

Now if the setting of P1 is changed to a higher value (say R2), the Triac turns on at firing angle $\theta2$ (where $\theta1 < \theta2$). The device turns on at a higher voltage when gate current is decreases by increasing the resistance offered by the potentiometer P1. Therefore the conduction period of the device is reduced to $(\pi - \theta2)$ and thus the average voltage across the load decreases compared to the earlier setting of potentiometer P1 (at R1) where R2>R1.

GSM

The aim of the project is to illustrate the various methods of interaction of Arduino Uno and the GSM (Global System for Mobile communication) cellular network using GSM TTL UART Modem (SIM 900A). With the GSM modem embedded with SIM 900A module, the Arduino board can do most of the operations such as make as well as receive voice calls, send and receive SMS, and connect to the internet over a GPRS network.

Components

- Arduino board
- GSM modem (SIM 900A)
- Battery (12V, 2A)
- Incandescent Lamp (100W, AC load)
- MOSFET (IRF540N)
- Resistance (1kΩ)
- Relay (12V)
- Breadboard

Project 23.1: Interfacing and Testing of GSM Module

The GSM module is controlled using AT commands through serial interface. The module is also equipped with I2C and SPI interface and supports communication in

850/ 900/ 1800/ 1900 MHz band. The module uses more current than the Arduino can supply (up to 2A), so we need an external high-current dc power supply of (5-12) V DC, 2A.

The following table provides the pin description of the GSM module.

Table 23.1: Technical specifications of SIM 900A

S.No	PIN	PIN NAME	DETAILS
1.	VIN	Input Voltage	(5-12)V DC, 2A
2.	GND	Ground	Ground Level for Input Voltage
3.	TXD	Transmit	Outputs data bytes– Connected to the RX pin of the Arduino
4.	RXD	Receive	Receives data bytes– Connected to the TX pin of the Arduino

The baud rate for the serial communication of the module is configurable between 1200 to 115200 through AT commands. Initially modem is in Auto-baud mode. This gives the flexibility to put the GSM module into operation with the Arduino board for a wide range of baud rates. The synchronization of baud rate between the module and Arduino is achieved by sending 'AT' character to the GSM module from the Arduino board. In response, the Arduino board receives 'OK' character from the module. The process of synchronization is a must before the Arduino board and the GSM module starts communicating with each other.

To establish a serial communication between Arduino and GSM module, the RX pin of the module must be connected to the TX pin of Arduino and TX pin of module to the RX pin of Arduino. The problem with this connection is that the programs will not be successfully uploaded to the Arduino board if the RX and TX pins of Arduino and module are connected during the process of uploading programs. So the RX and TX pins needs to be disconnected while uploading the program to Arduino board. Once the program is uploaded, reconnect the pins to start the operation.

To overcome this difficulty, two digital pins of Arduino are used for serial communication other than the RX and TX pins. This is made possible by using Software Serial Library of Arduino. Software Serial is a library of Arduino which enables serial data communication through other digital pins of Arduino. Digital pins 2 and 3 on Arduino board are used as virtual RX and TX serial lines to communicate with the GSM module.

Build the following circuit for testing the GSM module.

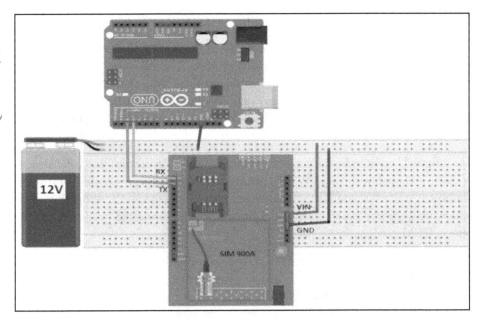

Figure 23.1: Interfacing GSM module and Arduino board wiring diagram

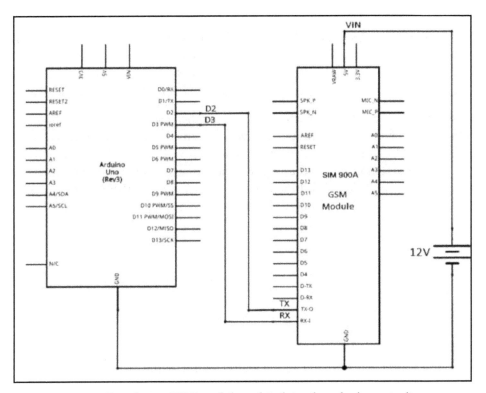

Figure 23.2: Interfacing GSM module and Arduino board schematic diagram

Explanation:

In the example, we want to display the details of the number (mobile phone) calling to the number (SIM) inserted in the GSM module. The following program can also be used for reference to ensure proper working of the setup. For this, digital pins 2 and 3 on Arduino board are used as virtual RX and TX serial lines to communicate with the GSM module. This also allows us to use serial monitor of Arduino to print the results.

The program begins by including 'SoftwareSerial' library. In the next line, a constructor of 'SoftwareSerial' with name 'GSM' is created and the digital pins 2 and 3 of Arduino are initialized as RX and TX SoftwareSerial port pins respectively. According to the schematic diagram, digital pin 2 and 3 of Arduino are connected to the TX and RX pins of GSM module.

Arduino is configured to perform two serial communications simultaneously with computer (through serial monitor) and also with the GSM module. To start the serial communication between Arduino and computer, we need to invoke 'Serial.begin' function at 9600 baud rate. Similarly serial communication is established between Arduino and GSM module by invoking 'GSM.begin' function both at 9600 baud rate.

The baud rate synchronization between Arduino and GSM module is achieved by sending an AT Command "AT". We also need to send the AT command "AT+CLIP=1" to display the number calling in. These AT commands are sent to the GSM module using 'GSM.println' function through software serial port (digital pins 2 and 3).

Now when we call the GSM module from another telephone, it sends back the information of the caller. Arduino receives the serial data through software serial port and holds the incoming character in character variable 'in_char'. On receiving a character, Arduino simultaneously prints the character on the Arduino IDE serial monitor as shown below. GSM module sends text 'NO CARRIER' after the call is hung up to the software serial port of Arduino.

Program:

```
#include <SoftwareSerial.h> // include SoftwareSerial library
SoftwareSerial GSM(2, 3); // create constructor 'GSM'
char in_char;

void setup()
{
Serial.begin(9600); // setting baud rate of serial monitor
GSM.begin(9600); // setting baud rate of GSM module
GSM.println("AT"); // for synchronization of Arduino and
GSM module
delay(100);
GSM.println("AT+CLIP=1\r"); // turn on caller identification
delay(100);
}

void loop()
{
if(GSM.available()>0) // checks for any data coming from
GSM module
{
in_char=GSM.read(); // read the incoming data from GSM
module
Serial.print(in_char); // print data to serial monitor of
Arduino
}
}
//end
```

Project 23.2: Receiving SMS text message in GSM Module

Next in this project we shall program the Arduino board to receive an SMS text message.

Explanation:

Inside the setup function, two AT commands are used to configure the GSM module for receiving SMS text message. First AT command used is "AT+CMGF" which sets SMS message format to text mode and the second command "AT+CNMI" configures the GSM module to send out the recent SMS message through its TX serial line.

The program inside the void loop function is similar to the earlier program for receiving a call. The while loop continues till a byte of data is available in the software serial port and simultaneously appends each character received to string variable 'in_string'. Once the program exists from the while loop, the whole string 'in_string' is displayed on the serial monitor as shown below.

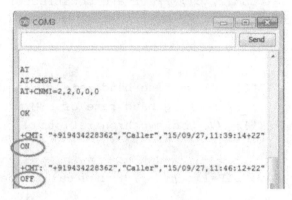

The text messages sent to the GSM module are strings "ON" and "OFF".

Program:

```
#include <SoftwareSerial.h> // include SoftwareSerial library
SoftwareSerial GSM(2, 3); // create constructor 'GSM'
String in_string="";
char in_char;

void setup()
{
pinMode(13, OUTPUT);
Serial.begin(9600); // setting baud rate of serial monitor
GSM.begin(9600); // setting baud rate of GSM module
GSM.println("AT"); // for synchronization of Arduino and
GSM module
delay(100);
GSM.println("AT+CMGF=1"); // set SMS message format to text
mode
delay(100);
GSM.println("AT+CNMI=2,2,0,0,0"); //new message indication
settings
}
void loop()
{
if(GSM.available()>0) //check whether data is available in
the software serial port
{
```

```
while(GSM.available()>0)  //continue  reading  data  from
software serial port
{
in_char=GSM.read(); //store the data in character variable
'in_char'
in_string=in_string + in_char; //append the character to
string 'in_string'
}
Serial.println(in_string); //print the complete string on
the serial monitor


}
}
//end
```

Project 23.3: Switching control of AC load through SMS Text Message

On extending the previous program, we can also control the switching of an AC load via SMS text message. On receiving a text message from the GSM module, the Arduino board turns ON or OFF an incandescent lamp and also sends an SMS back to the sender as an acknowledgement.

For switching ON and OFF an incandescent lamp, an important device used in the project is electromagnetic switch called relays. Relays are used for switching on and off electrical circuit at high AC voltage using a low DC voltage.

A SPDT (Single Pole Double Throw) 12V relay is used which has a total of five terminals. Two terminals are used to give the input DC voltage also known as the operating voltage of the relay. Relays are available in different operating voltages like 6V, 12V, 24V etc. The other three terminals are used to connect the high voltage AC circuit. These terminals are called Common, Normally Open (NO) and Normally Closed (NC).

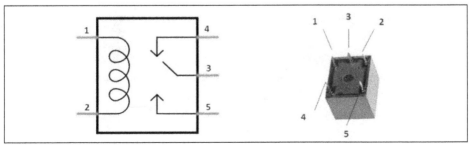

Figure 23.3: DC Relay and its wiring diagram

When the relay coil is inactive and not connected to any DC voltage, terminals 3 and 4 are normally closed whereas terminals 3 and 5 are normally open. On excitation of the relay coil with 12V DC supply across terminal 1 and 2, terminal 3 and 4 becomes open and 3 and 5 gets connected and acts as a closed switch.

The following table shows the pin description of a 12V DC relay.

Table 23.2: Relay pin description

Pin Number	Description
1 and 2	Relay Coil connection
3	Common terminal
4	Normally Closed terminal (NC)
5	Normally Open terminal (NO)

The table below illustrates about the ratings of a 12V DC relay.

Table 23.3: Relay specifications

S.No	Parameter	Value
1.	Rated Voltage	12V DC
2.	Rated Current	33.3mA
3.	Coil Resistance	360Ω
4.	Rated load voltage	250V
5.	Rated load current	12A
6.	Maximum switching power	3000VA

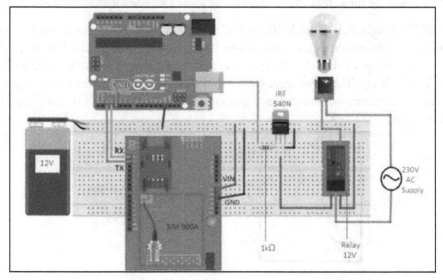

Figure 23.4: GSM module based AC load switching control wiring diagram

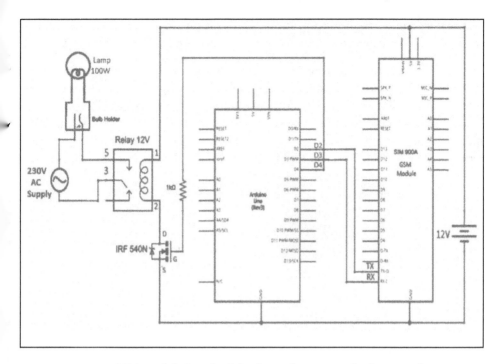

Figure 23.5: GSM module based AC load switching control schematic diagram

Explanation:

The setup functions in the sketch are same as the previous example however, digital pin 4 is also declared as output pin which controls the switching of the incandescent lamp. The 'get_number' function extracts the sender's mobile number using a very useful string function called 'substring'. Since the SMS text format is fixed, the statement 'in_string.substring(9, 22)' gets the characters from index 9 to 22 from string 'in_string' and stores the sender's mobile number in string variable 'number'.

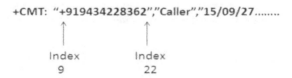

After getting the mobile number, we need to check the text message for turning ON or OFF the incandescent lamp. The program is written such that if the message contains string "ON" and "OFF", the lamp is turned ON and OFF respectively. This is checked using string function 'indexOf'.

The statement 'in_string.indexOf("ON")' checks for the occurrence of string "ON" in the string 'in_string' which holds the complete text message. If the string "ON" is present, the function returns the index value of the string else it returns integer value of

-1. On the event of the presence of string "ON", digital pin 4 is set HIGH to turn ON the MOSFET which causes the excitation of the relay coil and the lamp turns ON.

Similarly on occurrence of string "OFF" in the string variable 'in_string', the lamp is switched OFF by setting the digital pin 4 LOW. However, an acknowledgement text message is sent back to the sender's mobile number after every switching operation by calling 'send_msg' function. The AT command "AT+CMGS" is sent to the GSM module which tells the module to get ready to send a text message. The message is terminated by sending '26' to the GSM module which is the ASCII value of 'CTRL+Z'.

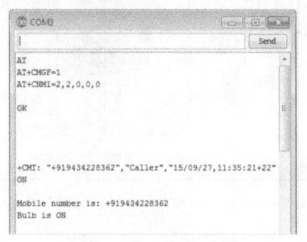

The figure below shows the screenshot of the SMS text conversation with the GSM module from the user's mobile phone.

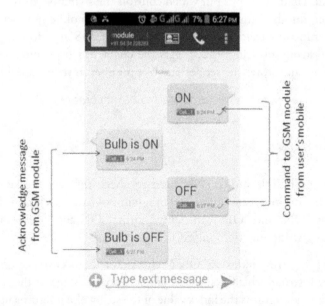

Program:

```
#include <SoftwareSerial.h> // include SoftwareSerial library
SoftwareSerial GSM(2, 3); // create constructor 'GSM'
String in_string="";
char in_char;
String number;
int status_on;
int status_off;

void setup()
{
pinMode(4, OUTPUT); // configure pin 4 as output to control
the swiitching
Serial.begin(9600); // setting baud rate of serial monitor
GSM.begin(9600); // setting baud rate of GSM module
GSM.println("AT"); // for synchronization of Arduino and
GSM module
delay(100);
GSM.println("AT+CMGF=1"); // set SMS message format to text mode
delay(100);
GSM.println("AT+CNMI=2,2,0,0,0"); //new message indication
settings
}

void loop()
{
if(GSM.available()>0) //check whether data is available in
the software serial port
{
while(GSM.available()>0)   //continue   reading   data   from
software serial port
{
in_char=GSM.read(); //store the data in character variable
'in_char'
in_string=in_string + in_char; //append the character to
string 'in_string'
}
Serial.println(in_string); //print the complete string on
the serial monitor
get_number(); //call function 'get_number()'
}

status_on=in_string.indexOf("ON"); //check whether "'ON"
is present in string 'in_string'
```

```
if(status_on!=-1) //string "ON" is present
{
digitalWrite(4, HIGH); //switch bulb ON
Serial.println("Bulb is ON"); // prints on the serial
monitor
send_msg("Bulb is ON");//call function 'send_msg' and pass
string "Bulb is ON"
}

status_off=in_string.indexOf("OFF"); //check whether "'OFF"
is present in string 'in_string'
if(status_off!=-1) //string "ON" is present
{
digitalWrite(4, LOW); //switch bulb ON
Serial.println("Bulb is OFF"); // prints on the serial monitor
send_msg("Bulb is OFF"); //call function 'send_msg' and
pass string "Bulb is ON"
}
in_string=""; //re-initialize string 'in_string' to null value
}

//function to get the mobile number
void get_number()
{
number=in_string.substring(9, 22); //extract the mobile
number from string 'in_string'
Serial.print("Mobile number is: ");
Serial.println(number); //prints the mobile number on the
serial monitor
}
//function to send acknowledgement message
void send_msg(String msg)
{
GSM.print("AT+CMGS="); //AT command to send text message
GSM.print('"');
GSM.print(number); //send mobile number to GSM module
GSM.println('"');
delay(1000);
GSM.print(msg); //send acknowledgement message to GSM module
GSM.write(26); //send ASCII code of 'CTRL+Z' to GSM module
}
//end
```

hapter Twenty Four

Arduino Standalone

This final project will guide us through the process of removing the microcontroller from the Arduino board and building a standalone microcontroller. In other words, we shall remove the Atmega 328 microcontroller from the Arduino UNO board and build a circuit which will function as the Arduino board. To make the Atmega 328 microcontroller work by itself we need some extra components as listed below.

Components

- Arduino board

- Crystal oscillator (16 MHz)

- Capacitor (22 pF)

- Resistor (10kΩ)

- Breadboard

Project 24.1: Building Standalone Circuit with Atmega 328

Before we proceed further, it is important for us to understand the pin diagram of Atmega 328. It is a 28 pin IC arranged in DIP and has 23 general purpose I/O lines. It has a maximum operating frequency of 20 MHz.

You need make sure that the microcontroller Atmega 328 is previously boot loaded. If you are having a new microcontroller, you need to upload the bootloader onto it. If the microcontroller already has the bootloader on it or if u took it out from the Arduino board then u can proceed with the further steps.

A bootloader is a small program that has been loaded on to the microcontroller and runs during start-up of the microcontroller. It helps in loading and running the programs in the microcontroller. Without the bootloader we'll not be able to upload and run any programs in the standalone microcontroller.

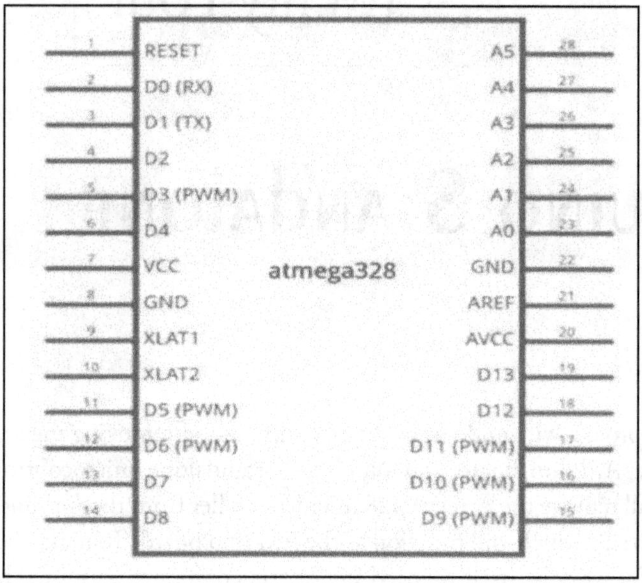

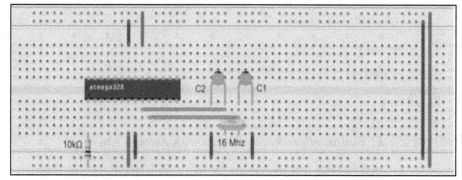

Figure 24.1: Atmega 328 pin diagram

For the microcontroller to work as a standalone device, we need a crystal clock of 16MHz, two capacitors of 22μF and a resistor of 10kΩ. Build the circuit shown below.

Figure 24.2: Atmega 328 standalone wiring diagram

Project 24.2: Uploading and Testing of Standalone Circuit

Now the above circuit on the breadboard can work as an independent microcontroller. Whenever we need to upload the programs on the microcontroller, we do it using the Arduino board. The circuit below (figure 24.4) shows the connection required for uploading the programs to the microcontroller. The program gets uploaded to the microcontroller on the breadboard through FTDI chip in the Arduino board.

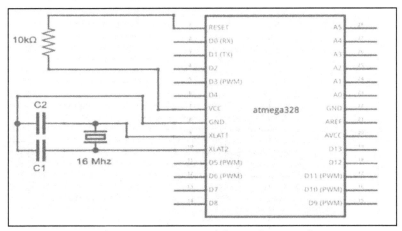

Figure 24.3: Atmega 328 standalone schematic diagram

Follow the connection listed in the table.

Table 24.1: Pin connections for uploading programs

Arduino Board Pins	Atmega 328 Pins
RESET	RESET
RX	RX
TX	TX
5V	VCC
GND	GND

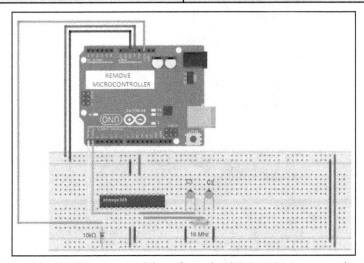

Figure 24.4: Atmega 328 standalone for uploading program wiring diagram

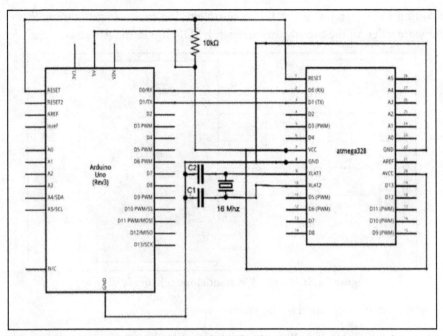

Figure 24.5: Atmega 328 standalone for uploading program schematic diagram

After uploading the Arduino sketch to the microcontroller, we can remove the connections to the Arduino pins RX, TX and RESET. Now the Arduino board is only used to supply power to the microcontroller on the bread board. The same can be done using an external battery of 9V.

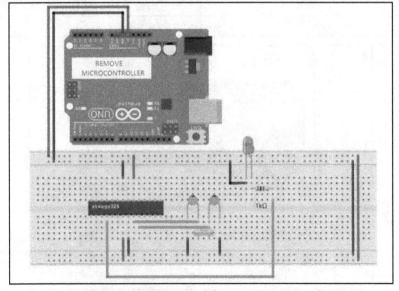

Figure 24.6: Atmega 328 standalone testing wiring diagram

Figure 24.6 can be used for testing the standalone circuit. After uploading the given program, the LED connected to pin 4 (D2) of Atmega 328 microcontroller should blink at an interval of one second.

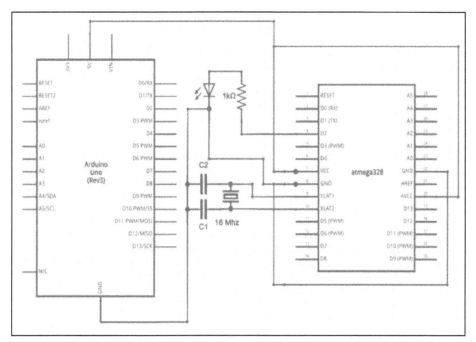

Figure 24.7: Atmega 328 standalone testing schematic diagram

Explanation:

The program turns the LED connected to pin 4 (D2) of Atmega 328 microcontroller ON and OFF for a period of one second each. This is the first test that can be done by the reader to verify the standalone circuit. This means we will now be able to build any of the previously discussed projects using standalone microcontroller. The advantage of this method is that it is cheaper compared to using the complete Arduino board and can also be used for autonomous projects.

Program:

```
int LED = 2;
void setup()
{
  pinMode(LED, OUTPUT); // initialize the digital pin as an
output.

}
```

```
void loop()
{
digitalWrite(LED, HIGH); // turn the LED on
delay(1000); // wait for a second
digitalWrite(LED, LOW); // turn the LED off
delay(1000); // wait for a second
}
//end
```

www.ingramcontent.com/pod-product-compliance
Lightning Source LLC
Chambersburg PA
CBHW071418050326
40689CB00010B/1885